THE VISUAL STORY

THE VISUAL STORY

CREATING THE VISUAL STRUCTURE OF FILM, TV AND DIGITAL MEDIA

SECOND EDITION

BRUCE BLOCK

Focal Press
Taylor & Francis Group

NEW YORK AND LONDON

First published 2008 by Focal Press
This edition published 2013
by Focal Press
70 Blanchard Road, Suite 402, Burlington, MA 01803

Simultaneously published in the UK
By Focal Press
2 Park Square, Milton Park, Abingdon, Oxon OX14 4RN

Focal Press is an imprint of the Taylor & Francis Group, an informa business

Notices

Practitioners and researchers must always rely on their own experience and knowledge in evaluating and using any information, methods, compounds, or experiments described herein. In using such information or methods they should be mindful of their own safety and the safety of others, including parties for whom they have a professional responsibility.

To the fullest extent of the law, neither the Publisher nor the authors, contributors, or editors, assume any liability for any injury and/or damage to persons or property as a matter of products liability, negligence or otherwise, or from any use or operation of any methods, products, instructions, or ideas contained in the material herein.

ISBN: 978-0-240-80779-9 (pbk)
ISBN: 978-0-080-55169-2 (ebk)

This book is dedicated to my parents,
Stanley and Helene Block.

CONTENTS

ACKNOWLEDGMENTS

I would like to thank my students at the University of Southern California and the thousands of other students and working professionals who have attended my classes and seminars at universities, film academies, advertising and design companies, and motion picture studios throughout the world. It is only through our interaction that this book has emerged.

No one finds his way alone. My teachers Word Baker, Lawrence Carra, Sulie and Pearl Harand, Dave Johnson, Bernard Kantor, Eileen Kneuven, Mordecai Lawner, William Nelson, Neil Newlon, Lester Novros, Woody Omens, Gene Peterson, Mel Sloan, Glenn Voltz, Jewell Walker, and Mort Zarkoff have inspired me, and continue to do so.

The practical aspects of making pictures that I discuss here are the outgrowth of working with talented professionals on commercials, documentaries, video games, Internet sites, animated and live-action television shows, and feature films. The experiences we shared have been critical to the maturation of the ideas presented in this book. I am particularly grateful to Bill Fraker, Neal Israel, and Charles Shyer, who helped give me my start in Hollywood.

Thanks to Dr. Rod Ryan for his astute comments about Chapter 6, "Color," Judith Kent and Brad Chisholm for their editorial notes, and Alan Mandel for the dialogue scene used in the appendix.

Much encouragement and support have come from Chris Huntley, Richard Jewell, Jane Kagon, Billy Pittard, Ronnie Rubin, my close friends Alan Dressler and Eric Sears, and my brother David Block.

A special thanks to Suzanne Dizon.

Bruce Block
Los Angeles, California 2007

INTRODUCTION

In Russia, on an icy winter night in 1928, an eager group of film students gathered in a poorly heated classroom at the Soviet GIK. The building, located on the Leningrad Chaussée, had once been the exclusive restaurant Yar, but was now the Russian Film Institute. Its main room with floor-to-ceiling mirrors and tall, white columns had become a lecture hall for the filmmaker and teacher Sergei Eisenstein. Eisenstein, Vsevolod Pudovkin, and Alexander Dovchenko were the first to develop formal theories of film structure based not only upon their own ideas but also on their practical experience making films.

Eisenstein's dual talents would take him all over the world. In 1933, he spoke at the Motion Picture Academy in Hollywood and lectured at the University of Southern California. He was only 50 when he died in 1948. Had Eisenstein lived, he might have met Slavko Vorkapich, a Yugoslavian filmmaker, who had been directing Hollywood montages at MGM, RKO, and Warner Bros. In the early 1950s Vorkapich briefly became chairman of the film department at USC. In his classes, he took Eisenstein's filmic ideas further, and developed groundbreaking theories about movement and editing. Vorkapich, with his charming, humorous teaching style, introduced fundamental cinematic concepts to new generations of filmmakers. He lectured internationally until his death in 1976.

In 1955, Lester Novros, a Disney artist, began teaching a class at USC about the visual aspects of motion pictures. His class was based on fine art theories and the writings of Eisenstein and Vorkapich. I took over teaching the course when Novros retired, and I decided to delve into his source material, including research in perception, psychology, the visual arts, theatre, and art history. It was my goal to bring film theory into the present, make it practical, and link it with story structure. I wanted to remove the wall between theory and practice so that visual structure would be easy to understand and use.

This book is the result of my experience in film and video production, coupled with my teaching and research. What you'll read in these pages can be used immediately in the preparation, production, and editing of theatrical motion pictures, television shows, short films, documentaries, commercials, computer games, Internet sites, and music videos, be it live action, animated, or computer generated. Whether you shoot on film or digital capture for a large, small, or tiny screen, the visual structure of your pictures often is overlooked, yet it's as important as the story you tell.

You will learn how to structure visuals as carefully as a writer structures a story or a composer structures music. Understanding visual structure allows you to communicate moods and emotions, give your production unity and style, and most importantly, find the critical relationship between story structure and visual structure.

Here, perhaps for the first time, you'll see how important the visual principles are to practical production. Some of these principles are thousands of years old; others are the result of new, emerging technologies.

The concepts in this book will benefit writers, directors, photographers, production designers, art directors, and editors who always are confronted by the same visual problems that have faced every picture maker. The students who sat in Eisenstein's cold Russian classroom had the same basic goal as the picture makers of today—to make a good picture. This book will teach you how to realize that goal.

CHAPTER

1

The Visual Components

The Cast of Visual Characters

Everywhere we go, we're confronted by pictures. We look at still pictures in books, magazines, and at museums. We watch moving pictures at the movies, on television, at concerts, and in theatres; we play video games and surf the Internet. We look at a lot of pictures—big, little, moving, still, color, or black and white—but they are all pictures.

This book is about learning how to understand and control these pictures.

Every picture is comprised of a story, visuals, and, sometimes, sounds. Used together, these three elements communicate the meaning of the picture to the viewer. If the picture is an advertisement, the viewer may be persuaded to purchase a product. If the picture is a computer game, the story, visuals, and sound can make the game addictive. If the picture is a movie, the viewer can become emotionally affected.

Pictures can be broken down into three fundamental building blocks:

- **Story**: Building blocks of plot, character, and dialogue

- **Sound**: Building blocks of dialogue, sound effects, and music

- **Visuals**: What are the building blocks of the visuals? Scenery? Props? Costumes? These answers are too limited—the building blocks for all visuals are the basic visual components.

The Basic Visual Components

The basic visual components are *space, line, shape, tone, color, movement,* and *rhythm.*

These visual components are found in every moving or still picture we see. Actors, locations, props, costumes, and scenery are made of these visual components. A visual component communicates moods, emotions, ideas, and most importantly, gives visual structure to the pictures. This book discusses these basic visual components in relation to television, computer, and movie screens, although these components are used in creating any picture.

SPACE

This is not outer space or "giving someone his or her space." There are three kinds of visual space: first, the physical space in front of the camera; second, the space as it appears on a screen; and third, the spatial size and shape of the screen itself.

LINE AND SHAPE

Line is a perceptual fact. It exists only in our heads. Line is the result of other visual components that allow us to perceive lines, but none of the lines we see is real. Shape goes hand in hand with line, because all shapes appear to be constructed from lines.

TONE

Tone refers to the brightness of objects in relation to the gray scale. Tone does not refer to the tone of a scene (sarcastic, excited, etc.), or to audio tone (treble and bass). Tone is an important factor in black & white and color photography.

COLOR

One of the most powerful visual components, color is also the most misunderstood. Basic color education is usually misleading and confusing. This book will simplify the complex component of color and make it simpler to understand and use.

MOVEMENT

Movement is the first visual component to attract the eye. Movement occurs using objects, the camera, and the viewers' eyes as they watch the screen.

RHYTHM

We're most familiar with rhythm we can hear, but there's also rhythm we can see. Rhythm is found in stationary (nonmoving) objects, moving objects, and editing.

Understanding and Controlling Visual Components

These are our cast of characters, the basic visual components: space, line, shape, tone, color, movement, and rhythm. Although we may be more familiar with the other cast called actors, both casts are critical to producing great work. Once production begins, the visual component cast will appear on-camera in every shot, communicating moods and emotions to the audience just like the actors. That's why understanding and controlling the visual components is so important.

Since actors have been introduced, we should take a moment to discuss them. An actor is a unique object to place on the screen. It is the actor's appearance, personality, and talent that attract an audience. The actor communicates by talking, making facial expressions, and using body language, but an actor is also a combination of spaces, lines, shapes, tones, colors, movements, and rhythms. So, in that respect, there's no difference between an actor and any other object.

Whether it is an actor, the story, the sound, or the visual components, audiences react emotionally to what they see and hear. Music easily communicates moods or emotions. Hitchcock's *Psycho* (1960) or Spielberg's *Jaws* (1975) demonstrate how music signals "terror" to the audience. In both films, music warns the audience that the murdering mother or the menacing shark is present. In *Psycho* it's the screech of the violins, and in *Jaws* it's the pounding notes of the bass. In both cases, the filmmaker introduces the musical theme when the murderous character first appears and then, by repeating that theme, reminds the audience of the threat. The music communicates fear, tension, and horror.

The same communication can occur using a visual component. Certain visual components already have emotional characteristics associated with them, although most of these visual stereotypes are easily broken. "Red means danger" is a visual stereotype. But green or blue could also communicate danger. Blue can mean "murder" to an audience, if it is properly defined for them. If every murder in a story occurs in blue light, the audience will expect a murder whenever blue light is presented to them. This is the concept used in Sidney Lumet's *Murder on the Orient Express* (1974). Once the blue color and its meaning are established, the audience accepts the idea and reacts accordingly.

In fact, any color can indicate danger, safety, good, evil, honesty, corruption, etc. Although stereotypes effectively prove that visual components can communicate with an audience, they're also the weakest, perhaps least creative use of the components. Visual stereotypes are often inappropriate, dated, and derivative. Any visual component can be used to communicate a wide range of emotions or ideas in new and interesting ways.

Can you decide not to use the visual components in your production? No; if you ignore the visual components, they won't go away. Color can be eliminated by shooting in black & white, but it's impossible to eliminate any other visual component, because they exist in everything on the screen. Even a blank screen contains the visual components of space, line, shape, tone, and movement. So the screen is never empty. Even a still photograph uses the components of rhythm and movement. Since the visual components are always on screen, understanding, controlling, and using them are critical to great picture making.

Defining the visual components opens the door to understanding visual structure, which can be a guide in the selection of locations, character design, colors, set dressing, props, typography fonts, wardrobe, lenses, camera positions, composition, lighting, actor staging, and editorial decisions. Understanding the visual components will answer questions about every visual aspect of your pictures.

Remember, though, that any study, if blindly adhered to, can be misleading. It's not the purpose of this book to leave you with a set of rigid textbook definitions and laws. If visual structure were that predictable anyone with a calculator could produce perfect pictures. Visual structure isn't math—it's not that predictable. Fortunately, there are some concepts, guidelines, and even some rules that will help you wrestle with the problems of producing a great visual production. The key is in the visual components.

In this book, I will explain each visual component. I'll describe it, illustrate it, and show you how to use it. The purpose of this book is to enable you to use visual structure and make better pictures.

Terms

This book will introduce some new ideas and terminology. The following are a few terms that need defining now.

THE SCREEN

The *screen* refers to the two-dimensional screens where we watch pictures. This includes movie screens, television and computer screens, screens on cell phones and other hand-held devices, the canvases hanging in museums, and the pages in books and magazines that display photographs and drawings. All of these two-dimensional surfaces are screens.

REAL WORLD/SCREEN WORLD

The *real world* is the environment in which we live. It's the three-dimensional place we inhabit. The *screen world* refers to images on any screen. It's the picture world we create with cameras, pencils, brushes, and computers. Sometimes the two different worlds will follow the same visual rules; other times they will not.

FOREGROUND, MIDGROUND, AND BACKGROUND

This book will use the term *foreground* abbreviated as FG (objects close to the viewer or camera), *midground* or MG (objects that are farther away from the viewer or camera), and *background* or BG (objects that are farthest away).

THE PICTURE PLANE

In this book, frame lines will surround anything visual in the screen world. These frame lines create a *picture plane*.

The picture plane is the "window" within which the picture exists. These frame lines represent the height and width of this window or screen. The proportions of the screen will vary, but every screen is a picture plane.

In a museum, the actual frame around the painting defines the picture plane. The picture plane of a camera is the viewfinder or the aperture of the film plane. The picture plane of a television or computer is the edges of the screen. When we hold our hands up in front of our eyes to frame a shot, we make a window with our hands. That, too, is a picture plane.

VISUAL PROGRESSION

Discussions about structure always lead to a discussion about progressions. A progression begins as one thing and changes to something else. Music can make a progression from slow to fast, for example. There are also visual progressions. The following visual progression begins with something simple and changes to something complex.

The simplest object we can place on a screen is a point. From here, the visual progression gains complexity.

The point can be moved across the screen creating a line. The line is visually more complicated than the point. The visual image has gained complexity.

If the line is pulled down, a plane is created. The two-dimensional plane is more complex than the line.

Chapter 1 • The Visual Components

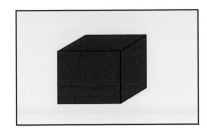

If the plane is moved out into space, the final and most complex level of this visual progression is created: a cube or volume.

This is a progression. From a point, to a line, to a plane, to a volume. From the simple to the complex. Visual structure, like any type of structure, uses progressions.

Practice, Not Theory

Right now you might be thinking that this book has made a sudden turn off the path of practicality. The introduction promised a book that would help you plan and shoot a movie or video. So what's all this "point, line, plane" stuff? Everything is sounding too theoretical.

Don't let these terms disillusion you. This book is about making better pictures, and controlling visual structure is critical to that goal. Visual theory will not ruin creative instincts, kill spontaneity, or become impractical. Visual structure is actually going to make your ideas work. Look at *Raging Bull* (1980) and you'll see that each boxing ring sequence is part of a progression that builds in story, sound, and visual intensity. Scorsese's fight sequences go from simple to complex. Or look for diagonal lines making the letter X in the opening shot of *The Departed* (2006) and watch for their recurrence throughout the film. In Hitchcock's *The Birds* (1963) there are visual progressions as the birds gather and attack. Watch the visual progression in the cornfield sequence in *North by Northwest* (1959).

Car commercials can make a vehicle appear faster than any other car on the market because the visual progressions are working. Watch any Fred Astaire or Busby Berkeley musical and you'll see visual progressions as the dance numbers increase in intensity. Look at the structural build at the end of Coppola's *The Godfather* (1972) when Michael Corleone takes control of the family business. Carefully planned visual progressions make the action sequences in *The Incredibles* (2004) build in intensity. Watch how the action sequences build from simple to complex in Spielberg's *Raiders of the Lost Ark* (1981), or follow how a nervous breakdown progresses visually in Roman Polanski's *Repulsion* (1965). Review *The Lord of the Rings* trilogy (2001–2003), which orchestrates its visual progressions during battle scenes.

Visual progressions make advanced levels of a video game gain intensity. David Fincher's *Seven* (1995) is a series of progressions that follow the crime scenes and add increasing intensity to each chase sequence. The color scheme in *American Beauty* (1999) is a consistent red, white, and blue. Watch the progressions of memory failure in *Eternal Sunshine of the Spotless Mind* (2004), and the color shifts in Eastwood's *Million Dollar Baby* (2004). If you know what to look for, they're all examples of solid story telling and visual progressions. They're all about visual structure.

A point becoming a line, developing into a plane, and changing into a volume is only a mechanical illustration of a visual progression that moves from something simple to something complex. Progressions are fundamental to story or musical structure, and they're fundamental to visual structure. Visual structure is controlled using the basic visual components and once these building blocks are explained, we'll explore visual structure and the critical link between the visuals and the story.

The first step is to take this cast of characters, called visual components, and discover who they are. It's a cast that we're stuck with, but it's a great cast. In fact, these seven cast members are capable of playing any part, any mood, any emotion, and they're great on television, a computer screen, or the big screen. This versatile cast works equally well in live action, animation, and computer-generated media. They're the most sought after (and least understood) players around.

Space, line, shape, tone, color, movement, and rhythm. Many picture makers don't even know what the visual components are, yet they've appeared in every film, television show, theatre performance, computer game, photograph, and drawing ever made. The visual components have no lawyers or agents, work for free, receive no residuals, and never arrive late. What better cast could you ask for?

Using the basic visual components requires an understanding of a key principle upon which all structure is based. This is the Principle of Contrast & Affinity, described in the next chapter.

2

Contrast and Affinity

The Key to Visual Structure

Visual structure is based on an understanding of the Principle of Contrast & Affinity. What is contrast? Contrast means difference.

Here's an example of contrast using the visual component of tone. Tone refers to the brightness of objects. Tone can be organized using a gray scale. Contrast of tone means two shades of gray that are as different in terms of brightness as possible. The two gray tones with maximum contrast or difference are the black square and the white square. A picture illustrating maximum contrast of tone would use only black and white tones.

This shot, all black and white, is an example of maximum contrast of tone.

What is affinity? Affinity means similarity.

Any gray tones next to each other on the gray scale have affinity. A picture illustrating maximum affinity of tone would use a limited portion of the gray scale.

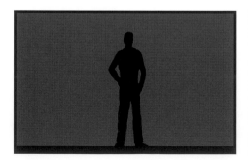 

These shots are examples of tonal affinity. One uses only black and dark gray, and the other shot uses two light gray tones.

Every visual component (space, line, shape, tone, color, movement, and rhythm) can be described and used in terms of contrast and affinity, which we'll discuss in the chapters that follow.

To put it simply, contrast means difference and affinity means similarity.

The Principle of Contrast & Affinity states:

The greater the contrast in a visual component, the more the visual intensity or dynamic increases. The greater the affinity in a visual component, the more the visual intensity or dynamic decreases.

More simply stated:

Contrast = Greater Visual Intensity

Affinity = Less Visual Intensity

What does *visual intensity* mean? A state-of-the-art rollercoaster ride is intense; a sleeping puppy is not. A wild action sequence in a great movie is exciting; a picture of a calm ocean shore on an overcast day is not. A computer game can be exciting or dull. A television commercial can be agitating or soothing. A documentary can be alarming or reassuring. These emotional reactions are based on the intensity, or dynamic, of the audience's emotional reaction when they read a book, listen to music, or see a picture. The audience's reaction can be emotional (they cry, laugh, or scream) or physical (their muscles tense up, they cover their eyes, they fall asleep). Usually the more intense the visual stimulus, the more intense the audience reaction.

A good writer carefully structures words, sentences, and paragraphs. A good musician carefully structures notes, measures, and bars. A director, cinematographer, production designer, or editor structures visuals by applying the Principle of Contrast & Affinity to the basic visual components.

The effect of the Principle of Contrast & Affinity can be demonstrated with a simple drawing:

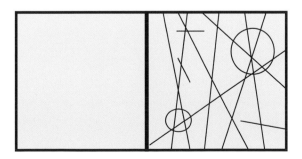

Which half of this frame is more intense? The right half is full of contrasting lines that create visual intensity. The left half lacks intensity due to the visual affinity. Each half of the frame has a different visual personality.

Here's another example using two hypothetical short films:

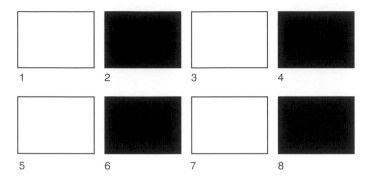

1   2   3   4

5   6   7   8

This is a storyboard for the first film. A storyboard is a set of drawings that illustrate what the final film will look like. Each shot in this film lasts one second. The frame starts white and then goes black, then white, black, etc. This alternation of white and black will continue for several minutes. The audience's response is fairly predictable. The rapid assault of contrasting black and white frames will become too intense and impossible to watch. The film is all contrast; it is too intense.

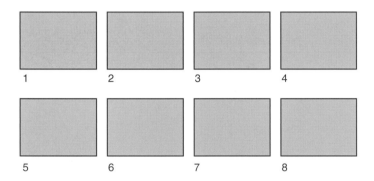

1   2   3   4

5   6   7   8

This is a storyboard for the second film. Every frame is the same gray tone; nothing changes. The audience will watch this movie for several minutes and, of course, find it dull and monotonous. The film is all affinity. It lacks visual dynamic.

The contrast of the white/black movie is too intense, and the affinity of the gray movie has no intensity at all.

Although the Principle of Contrast & Affinity is simple, using it gets complicated. Each of the seven basic visual components can be broken down into various subcomponents, and all of them must be related back to contrast and affinity. But once the basic visual components and the Principle of Contrast & Affinity are understood, controlling visual structure becomes possible.

The next six chapters define the basic visual components. It is critical to know how to see them, control them in practical production, and, most importantly, use them to build a visual structure.

3

Space

space is a complex visual component. It not only defines the screen where all the other visual components are seen, but space itself has several subcomponents that must be explained. This chapter is divided into two parts. Part One defines the four subcomponents of space: deep, flat, limited, and ambiguous. Part Two discusses aspect ratio, surface divisions, and open and closed space.

PART ONE: THE PRIMARY SUBCOMPONENTS

The real world that we live in is three-dimensional, having height, width, and depth. But the physical nature of a screen is strictly two-dimensional. Movie, television, and computer screens are flat surfaces that can be measured in height and width but, practically speaking, have no depth.

The challenge is to portray our three-dimensional world on a two-dimensional screen surface and have the result appear believably three-dimensional. A viewer should watch the screen's two-dimensional pictures and accept the images as a realistic representation of our three-dimensional world.

How can a two-dimensional screen surface display pictures that appear to have three dimensions or depth? The answer is not 3D movies or holograms (although the latter is truly a three-dimensional picture). Pictures can appear three-dimensional even though they're being viewed on flat two-dimensional screen surfaces.

Deep Space

Deep space is the illusion of a three-dimensional world on a two-dimensional screen surface. It's possible to give an audience the visual experience of seeing a three-dimensional space (height, width, and depth), even though all the depth is illusory. There is never real depth because the screen upon which the picture exists is only two-dimensional.

The audience believes they see depth on a two-dimensional screen because of depth cues.

This is a picture of busy freeway that stretches far into the distance. The cars in the right lanes race away from camera, and the cars on the left come from the distance, and move quickly past the camera. This description seems correct, but it's completely wrong. The picture is being displayed on a flat two-dimensional piece of paper (or a flat screen) so there can't be any real depth. Still, we believe that the freeway extends into the depth of the picture, and that some of the cars are closer, and others are farther away. There is something about this two-dimensional picture that convinces us we're seeing depth, where there's no actual depth at all. That something is called a depth cue.

The Depth Cues

Deep space, the illusion of depth on a two-dimensional surface, is created and controlled using the depth cues. Depth cues are visual elements that create the illusion of depth.

Perspective

The most important depth cue is perspective. When creating illusory depth for a flat screen, it is essential to know how to recognize perspective in the real world.

Here's the two-dimensional plane that was introduced in Chapter 1. The plane's top and bottom lines are parallel and its left and right side lines are parallel. This is a frontal plane.

This wall is the same as the frontal plane. Visually, the frontal plane and the wall have no depth but they can be given the appearance of depth by adding perspective. For our purposes, perspective comes in three basic types: one-point, two-point, and three-point perspective.

One-Point Perspective

This is the simplest type of perspective.

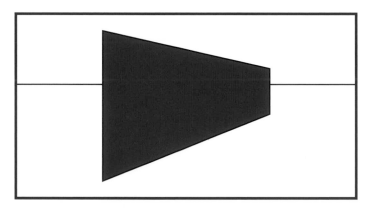

Using the same wall, the viewer's position can be moved, revealing the depth cue of perspective.

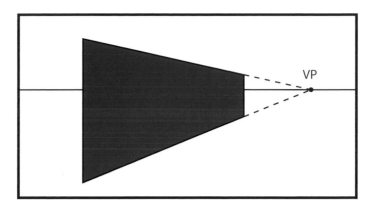

The lines along the top and bottom of the plane now appear to meet or converge at a single point called a vanishing point or VP. Usually the vanishing point appears on the horizon, although it can appear anywhere. This creates a longitudinal plane, an extremely important cue to illusory depth. The longitudinal plane appears to have depth. One side of the plane looks farther away even though it exists on this flat paper surface.

A classic example of one-point perspective occurs when standing in the middle of a railroad track. The rails appear to meet or converge at a vanishing point on the horizon. The rails never actually meet; they always remain parallel, but they appear to converge toward the vanishing point.

The rails of the train track create a longitudinal plane. This longitudinal plane would extend to the horizon, but in the diagram, the plane is shortened for clarity. We equate this convergence with distance. The more the rails converge, the farther away they seem.

Convergence occurs in the real world and in the screen world, but in the screen world it happens on a two-dimensional surface, and is a cue to illusory depth. The railroad tracks seem to go into the depth of the picture, but there is no real depth on a flat screen.

Two-Point Perspective

The next, more complex, level is two-point perspective, which uses two vanishing points. There are several ways that two-point perspective can be produced, shown here:

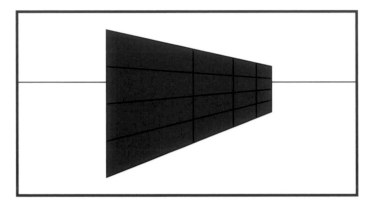

This longitudinal plane still has only one vanishing point. Additional lines have been added to the plane to make the convergence more obvious.

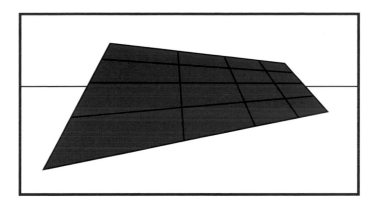

The longitudinal plane can be given a second vanishing point. If the viewing position is raised or lowered, the sides of the longitudinal plane no longer remain parallel.

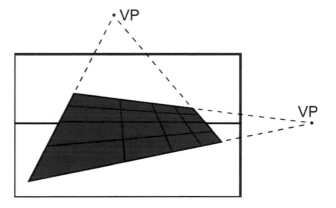

There are two vanishing points. The plane's top and bottom lines converge to one vanishing point located to the left of the frame. The sides of the plane converge to a second vanishing point located above the frame. If the viewing position is raised, the sides of the longitudinal plane will converge to a vanishing point below the frame.

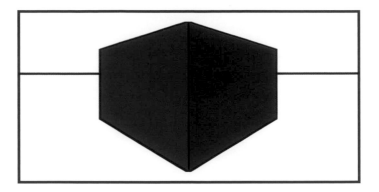

Two vanishing points can also be generated using two separate longitudinal surfaces.

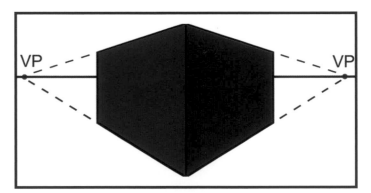

Commonly, this occurs at the corners of buildings. The top and bottom lines of each longitudinal plane converge to separate vanishing points.

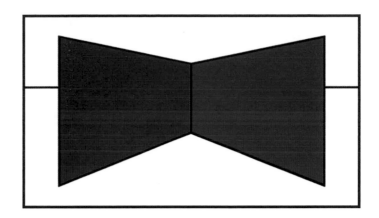

Inverting the two longitudinal planes reveals another example of two-point perspective. This occurs when looking into the corner of a room, for example.

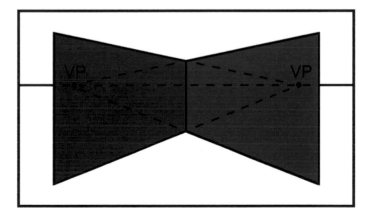

Although the vanishing points are hidden behind the longitudinal planes, there are still converging lines.

Three-Point Perspective

Three-point perspective is more complex than one- or two-point perspective. Examples are shown in the following pictures.

This is a view of a tall building. All the lines in the building will converge to one of three vanishing points.

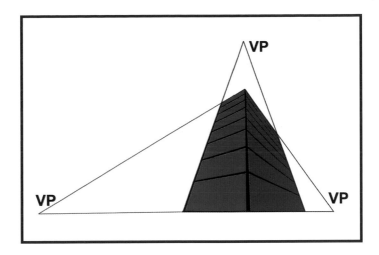

One vanishing point will appear above the building. The second and third vanishing points will appear along the horizon line to the building's left and right.

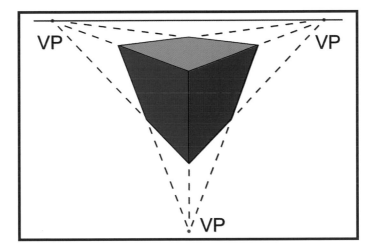

This shot also illustrates three-point perspective, but the viewing position is above the building.

Perspective, vanishing points, and longitudinal planes can be applied to any object in the real world, as the following pictures illustrate.

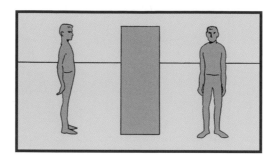

When the camera is at eye level, an actor is like a flat, frontal plane.

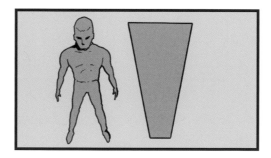

When the camera is lowered and tilted up, the actor becomes a longitudinal plane. This also occurs when the camera is raised and tilted down at the actor.

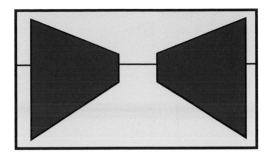

The audience's attention will usually be drawn to any on-screen vanishing point. Notice how your eye is drawn to the vanishing point between the two walls.

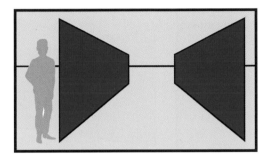

In this picture the viewer's attention is drawn to the actor, but it's also drawn to the vanishing point between the two walls.

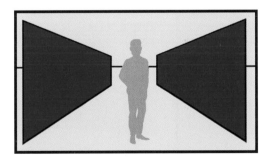

Here, with the actor repositioned at the vanishing point between the two walls, the viewer's attention goes to the actor. The vanishing point helps keep the audience's attention on the actor.

Does this mean that actors must always be located on the vanishing point? Absolutely not. But it's important to know that vanishing points will usually attract an audience's attention.

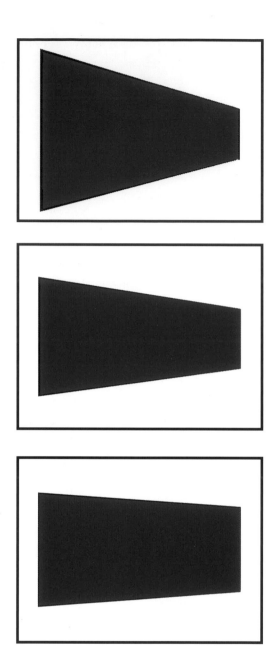

As a vanishing point moves out of frame, its ability to attract the audience's attention decreases.

Moving from one-, two-, and three-point perspective is a visual progression. The more vanishing points, the greater the illusion of depth. One vanishing point will create the illusion of depth, but adding a second or third point will enhance the illusion of deep space.

It's possible to use four, five, twenty, or more vanishing points in a picture. If this were a drawing exercise (and it isn't) we'd spend time learning the complexities of multiple point perspective. But an audience watching a movie or video doesn't notice more than three vanishing points. This limitation is an advantage for the picture maker because it means there are only three levels of illusory depth possible when using perspective and convergence.

Remember that no matter how many vanishing points are added, there isn't any real depth. The drawings and photographs used here to illustrate deep space exist on a flat, two-dimensional page surface. All the depth is illusory.

Size Difference

As an object of known size gets smaller, it appears farther away. As an object of known size gets larger, it appears closer.

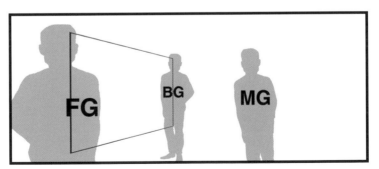

This shot has depth because the three people have been staged on three separate planes. One is on the FG (foreground) plane, another on the MG (midground) plane, and the third is on the BG (background) plane. Separating the objects onto FG, MG, and BG planes increases their size difference. Also notice how the FG and BG person create a longitudinal plane. Of course, all three people are exactly the same distance away because they're on the same flat surface (this page). The size change creates the illusion of depth.

This concept might seem simple and obvious, but size difference is an extremely important method of creating illusory depth on a flat surface. In Orson Welles' *Citizen Kane* (1941), the staging of actors and the illusion of depth are based primarily on perspective and size change. In fact, this depth cue is sometimes called *staging in depth*.

Movement

Illusory depth is created by moving an object in front of the camera, or by moving the camera itself. Later in Chapter 7, the concept of movement will be expanded into other areas.

Object Movement

An object is anything in front of the camera: a person, an animal, a basketball, a chair, a car, a boat, a beam of light; it makes no difference.

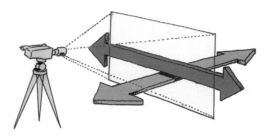

There are only two basic directions that an object in the real world can move in front of the camera. The object can either move *parallel* or *perpendicular* to the picture plane. Remember that the picture plane is the two-dimensional "window frame" within which pictures exist.

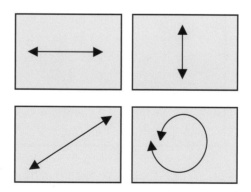

Movement parallel to the picture plane can be left-right, up-down, diagonal, or in a circular direction.

A single object moving parallel to the picture plane cannot create depth, but deep space is created on a flat screen surface when two or more objects in different planes move parallel to the picture plane.

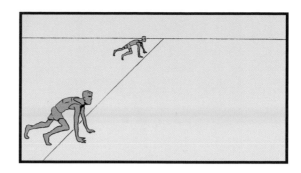

This example shows two track runners (one in the FG and one in the BG) at a starting line. Both runners will begin running at the same time parallel to the picture plane, and move at identical speeds. But the FG runner will appear to move across the picture plane faster than the BG runner, even though both runners actually travel the same distance.

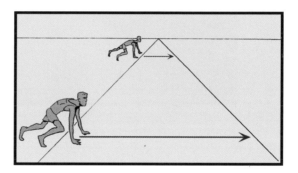

Adding a vanishing point accurately diagrams how much farther the FG runner appears to move even though both runners actually travel the same distance. As the viewer compares the apparently slower speed and shorter movement of the BG runner to the FG runner, the viewer believes the BG runner is farther away (the BG runner is also smaller, which adds depth). The apparent difference in speed and distance traveled produces the depth cue called relative movement.

Illusory depth is also created when an object moves perpendicular to the picture plane. Objects that move toward or away from the camera are moving perpendicular to the picture plane. Perpendicular movement ranges from moving directly at the camera to moving at a diagonal in depth across the frame.

As an object moves at a constant speed toward the camera it appears to increase in speed. Conversely, as an object moves away from the camera it appears to slow down. This change in apparent speed is the depth cue produced by movement perpendicular to the picture plane. For example, as an airplane taxis down a runway and takes off, it actually gains speed, but it appears to slow down as it flies away into the distance.

Camera Movement

There are three camera moves that create relative movement and illusory depth. These moves are the dolly in/out, the track left/right, and the boom up/down. It doesn't matter how the camera is being moved (by dolly, crane, car, helicopter, special mechanical rigs, or simply hand-held)—the same basic principles apply.

A dolly in/out means moving the camera closer or farther from a subject. A dolly creates relative movement between the FG and the BG.

As the camera dollies in, the FG actor will get larger faster than the two actors in the BG. This is due to the relative distances of the FG and BG actors from the camera.

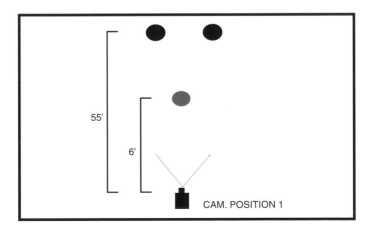

An overhead view or ground plan map will explain the answer. The camera begins 6 feet from the FG actor and 55 feet from the BG actors.

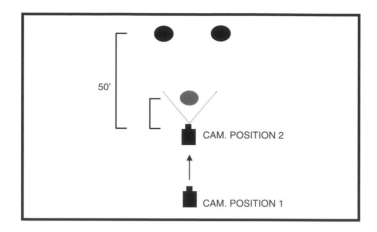

The camera dollies in 5 feet. Now the camera is only 1 foot from the FG actor, and 50 feet from the BG actors. The FG actor is now six times closer to the camera, so there is a large size increase in the FG actor. The BG actors moved from 55 feet to 50 feet from the camera (only 1/10th closer), so their size change is minimal.

This relative difference in size change during the camera move creates depth. The FG object moves faster than the BG object, creating relative movement.

Conversely, when the camera dollies out (away from the subject), the FG actor will quickly decrease in size and the BG actors will barely change size at all. The relative movement between the BG and FG is the cue to depth.

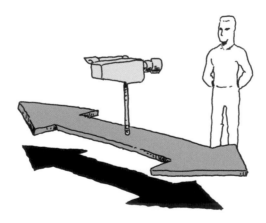

Illusory depth can also be created when a camera dollies left and right, sometimes called a tracking shot.

This shot uses a FG actor and three BG actors. The camera dollies to the right.

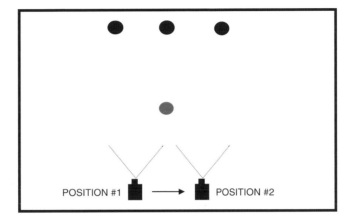

As the camera dollies or tracks from left to right, the FG actor passes the camera faster than the three actors in the BG. There's relative movement between the faster moving FG and the slower moving BG objects. An audience interprets the relative movement between the FG and the BG as a depth cue.

The third camera move that produces illusory depth is a boom or crane shot.

The camera is raised or lowered, usually on a mechanical arm.

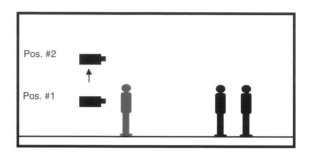

The shot uses one FG actor and two BG actors. As the camera cranes up, the actor in the FG will pass quickly out the bottom of the frame, and the BG actors will move down more slowly. As the camera cranes down, the FG actor will come into the frame quickly, but the BG actors will barely move.

The crane shot produces the same kind of relative movement created by the tracking shot, but instead of generating horizontal relative movement, the crane shot produces vertical relative movement.

In all three cases, the movement of the camera creates relative movement in the objects. It is the relative movement that creates the illusion of depth on the flat, two-dimensional screen.

Textural Diffusion

Every object has texture and detail. A plain plaster wall has a smooth texture with almost no detail, and a wool sweater has a nubbley texture with a lot of textural detail. Depth created by differences in textural detail is called textural diffusion.

This photograph illustrates textural diffusion. The fans in the FG seats have individual textures and details. The fans sitting in the BG are reduced to tiny dots, and their individual textural detail is gone. Objects showing more textural detail appear closer, and objects with less detail appear farther away. This photo also incorporates other depth cues like size change and perspective. As each new depth cue is explained, the overlapping characteristics of the cues will become apparent.

Aerial Diffusion

Aerial diffusion depends on particles in the air. These particles can be dust, fog, rain, smog, smoke, or anything suspended in the air that obscures the view of the BG.

Aerial diffusion causes three visual changes in a picture that create the illusion of depth. The aerial diffusion causes a loss in detail and texture, it lowers the picture's tonal contrast, and it changes the color of objects to the color of the aerial diffusion itself.

On a clear day without aerial diffusion in the air (no smog, fog, rain, mist, etc.), we might say that the view looks "sparkling" or "clear." What we're describing is the abundance of textural detail and uncontaminated color that is visible on days when there isn't any aerial diffusion.

The visual quality is completely different on a foggy day. The aerial diffusion is now adding depth cues to the picture. The details of the buildings are gone, and there is an overall lack of tonal contrast. Very bright and very dark building colors are replaced with middle grays.

Fog also changes the color of objects to gray (the color of the aerial diffusion). If the aerial diffusion were brown smog, the distant building would have turned brown. The aerial diffusion obscures the textural detail, lowers the tonal contrast, and changes the color of objects in the shot.

For aerial diffusion to be an effective depth cue, there must be an object unaffected by the aerial diffusion and another object affected by the aerial diffusion in the same shot. The comparison between the two objects creates the depth.

The loss of textural detail due to aerial diffusion seems similar to textural diffusion, but the causes are different. Textural diffusion relies on actual distance to produce a loss in detail. Aerial diffusion does not rely on actual distance but rather on particles in the air, which obscure textural detail and make the object seem farther away.

Shape Change

An object's shape change is perceived as a cue to illusory depth. Shape change can occur on moving objects or stationary (nonmoving) objects.

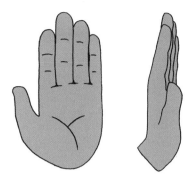

Here are two pictures of a hand.

Reducing the hands to silhouettes shows that the same hand can have different shapes.

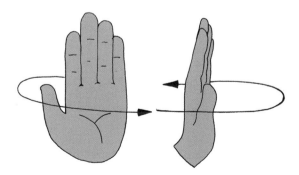

In the real world the hand changes shape by turning in space. Any turning object needs a third dimension that allows the object rotation to occur. As an object turns in the real world it changes shape in the screen world. This shape change is a cue to illusory depth.

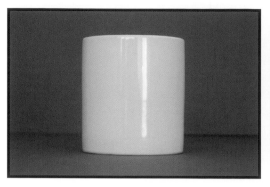 

A cup, for example, changes shape as it turns or as the camera moves around it. From table height, it appears as a rectangle but when viewed from above it's a circle. Almost all objects change shape (silhouette) as they turn, or as the camera moves around the object in three-dimensional space.

Shape change also occurs without movement. This picture of a building appears deep because it uses a longitudinal surface, size difference (the windows get smaller), and because the windows change shape.

BOTTOM WINDOWS   TOP WINDOWS

In the photograph, the lower windows appear tall and rectangular, and the upper windows appear as short, squat rectangles. This change in shape is a cue to illusory depth. The viewer assumes all the windows are actually the same shape, so an apparent shape change is interpreted as depth.

Tonal Separation

Tone refers to black and white and the gray scale. The gray scale contains no color. It's a series of tonal steps from black to white. Tonal separation deals with a viewer's perception of depth due to the brightness of objects. Usually, lighter objects appear closer and darker objects appear farther away.

This is the gray scale.

Even with two objects of identical size, a viewer will usually see the brighter object as closer and the darker object as farther away .

Color Separation

Colors can be used as a depth cue by classifying them into warm and cool groups. The warm colors are red, orange, and yellow, and the cool colors are blue and green. Chapter 6, "Color," elaborates on this list and explains the complexities of color more fully.

Warm colors usually seem closer to the viewer and cool colors appear farther away.

The red rectangle seems closer and the blue rectangle appears farther away, even though both are the same distance from the viewer.

There are many theories about why this happens. Researchers believe it's linked to human physiological and psychological responses to different wavelengths of light. Whatever the reason, the perceptual fact exists and can be used to create illusory deep space on a flat screen surface.

Up/Down Position

The vertical location of objects in the frame affects their apparent distance from the viewer. Objects higher in the frame appear farther away, and objects lower in the frame seem closer.

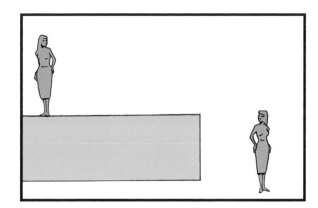

Even though these two people are the same size, a viewer will perceive the person lower in the frame to be more in the FG.

If there is a horizon line in the frame, the up/down position depth cue becomes more complex. Objects closer to the horizon will appear more distant and objects farther from the horizon will seem closer.

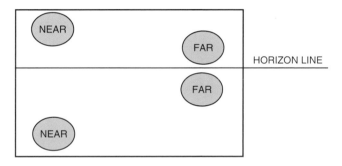

Below the horizon, objects higher in the frame seem farther away. The opposite is true above the horizon where objects higher in the frame appear closer.

Overlap

When one object overlaps another, illusory depth is created.

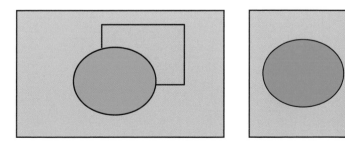

In the first shot, the square appears farther away because the circle covers or overlaps part of the square. The overlapping creates depth because one object must be closer than the other object for the overlap to occur.

The overlapping objects create more depth than the objects without overlap. In most cases, overlap is a minor depth cue. The overlapping objects must display other major depth cues before the actual overlap adds much illusory depth.

Focus

Focus refers to the sharpness of objects in a picture.

Objects can be in sharp focus or blurred. As a depth cue goes out of focus, it loses its deep space characteristics and becomes flat or limited space (both are discussed later in this chapter). A blurred BG may appear more distant from an in-focus FG, but the result is not deep space. A depth cue can be effective only if it is in focus.

3D Pictures

The first stereoscopic pictures, drawings actually, appeared in the early 1830s. As soon as photography was invented, stereoscopic photographs appeared everywhere. The first 3D movie was shown in 1915 and since then, producers and exhibitors have used it in a variety of viewing situations. The parallax created by two screen images, one being viewed by each eye, can create a realistic sense of depth. The variables of interocular distance, point of convergence, and lens focus each play an important role in determining the amount of deep space the audience will perceive.

3D works best when it is used in conjunction with the depth cues that are discussed in this chapter. Without them, the 3D experience is unsatisfying because the real world cues we're used to experiencing aren't present in the 3D images. Our real world reliance on the depth cues is so strong that without them, the sense of deep space is diminished.

Flat Space

Flat space is the opposite of deep space. Deep space gives the illusion of a three-dimensional picture on a two-dimensional screen surface. Flat space is not an illusion. Flat space emphasizes the two-dimensional quality of the screen surface. This creates a completely different kind of visual space. Chapter 9, "Story and Visual Structure," will show how to use and give meaning to all the types of space discussed in this chapter.

The Flat Cues

Just as deep space has specific cues to create illusory depth, flat space has its own cues. In creating flat space, the depth cues must be eliminated and replaced with flat space cues.

Frontal Planes

Perspective, converging lines, and vanishing points must be eliminated in flat space.

Planes must be frontal, not longitudinal. Here is the frontal plane that was introduced earlier in this chapter.

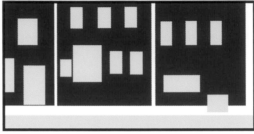

The frontal plane emphasizes the two-dimensionality of the screen surface. The diagram reveals the frontal surfaces in the photograph. There are no longitudinal surfaces and the vanishing points have been eliminated.

Size Constancy

To emphasize the flatness or two-dimensionality of the screen, all similarly sized objects should be kept the same size and staged on the same frontal plane.

Flat space requires staging objects on a single plane that is parallel to the picture plane. The single frontal plane created by the staging emphasizes the two-dimensional screen surface.

Movement

Both object movement and camera movement can be used to create flat space.

Object Movement

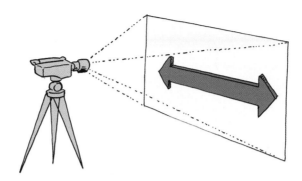

In flat space, objects move parallel to the picture plane.

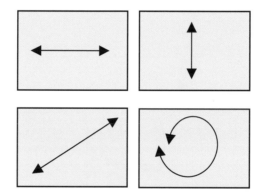

This parallel movement can be side to side, up and down, diagonally, or in a circle.

An actor walking parallel to the picture plane emphasizes flat space. Movement perpendicular to the picture plane should be avoided because it activates too many depth cues. An exception to this rule, movement perpendicular to the picture plane photographed with a telephoto lens, is discussed in the next section of this chapter.

Camera Movement

There are three camera moves that maintain flat space because they do not create relative movement: the pan, the tilt, and the zoom.

The camera pan creates flat space.

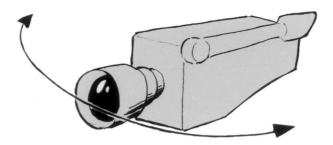

Panning means rotating the camera to the left or right on its horizontal axis. When the camera pans, all objects in the frame keep their relative positions to one another. There is no relative movement.

The tilt is the second flat space camera move.

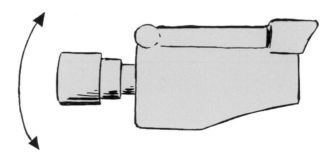

Tilting moves the camera on a vertical axis. There is no relative movement created with a tilt. True panning and tilting occur when the camera is mounted on its nodal point, which is explained in the appendix.

Finally, there's the zoom. A zoom is not really a camera move, but it is the flat space equivalent of the deep space dolly. Many cinematographers and directors have strong negative opinions about the zoom. Typically, they feel that the zoom is a quick, unattractive way to achieve a dolly shot. It's true that a dolly shot will take longer to set up than a zoom shot, but the difference is not just economical or practical. The difference is in the type of visual space that the zoom or dolly produces.

A zoom creates flat space for a number of reasons. Most importantly, the camera is not physically moving, so there will be no relative movement. A zoom-in enlarges everything in the frame at exactly the same rate of speed. The FG, MG, and BG grow larger in unison as if everything in the picture existed on a single, flat plane. Relative movement is eradicated. A zoom-in also alters the focal length of the lens, changing it from a wider angle to a telephoto lens. As the focal length of the lens increases, the depth of field decreases so areas of the frame will go out of focus. As any object blurs, it becomes flat.

When zooming in, all objects, regardless of their distance from the camera, increase in size at exactly the same rate. Depth of field decreases, so more of the picture becomes out of focus. Out-of-focus objects, no matter what depth cues they contain, read as flat space. Zooming out also eliminates relative movement, and even though depth of field increases, the zoom-out itself does not add depth to the picture.

Flat space demands that the deep space camera moves (dolly in/out, tracking left/right, and cranes) are avoided. However, there is an exception when it's possible to maintain flat space by using a tracking shot.

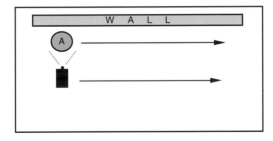

In this illustration, an actor (A) walks along a wall and the camera dollies next to the actor. The camera is dollying parallel to the frontal plane of the wall, which will keep its surface frontal and flat.

It is also possible to maintain flat space when an object moves perpendicular to the picture plane, but there are restrictions for the lens choice and the distance of the object from the camera.

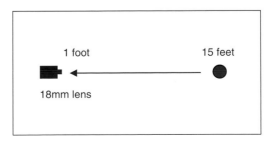

In this situation the camera uses a wide-angle 18mm lens. An actor walks toward the camera from 15 feet away. As the actor moves toward the camera too many depth cues will be activated. Size change, textural detail, and speed change will all create deep space.

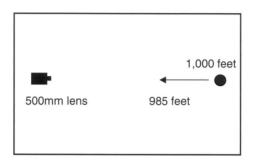

Now, the actor begins 1,000 feet away, walks 15 feet, and stops 985 feet from the camera. The actor moved the same 15-foot distance toward the camera but none of the depth cues appears. This is true for any lens, although this example uses a telephoto lens. Because the actor remains so far from the camera, there will be no size change, detail gain, or increase in the object's speed. Even though the actor is moving perpendicular to the picture plane, there won't be any depth cues activated, because there is so little difference between 1,000 feet and 985 feet from the camera. The relative distance between the camera and the actor remains nearly constant, so flat space will be maintained.

Textural Diffusion

Objects without texture look farther away, and heavily textured objects appear closer. To achieve flat space, avoid these differences because it creates depth.

To emphasize flat space, all objects must have the same amount of textural detail. A flatter space is produced when there's a homogenization, or similarity of texture, throughout the picture. Maintaining flat space by manipulating FG and BG texture is difficult, but avoiding heavily textured FG objects can aid in maintaining flat space.

The texture in the shot is similar throughout. There are many flat space cues but the heavily textured BG tends to move forward and flatten the space.

Aerial Diffusion

Aerial diffusion can create flat space if the diffusion overwhelms all the depth cues in the picture.

Although aerial diffusion can be a depth cue, here the aerial diffusion (falling snow) has eliminated the detail and texture from the entire picture. Most of the shot lacks texture and contrast, and is the same color. This creates flat space.

Shape Change

In creating a strictly flat space, objects should never change shape. A flat, graphic animated film can accomplish this, but eliminating shape changes due to turns and rotations in a three-dimensional, real world space is extremely difficult. A picture maker might minimize shape change, but eliminating it is impossible.

Tonal Separation

Tone refers to the gray scale. Maintaining flat space requires a reduction of the gray scale range within the picture. Remember, brighter objects usually appear closer and darker objects seem farther away.

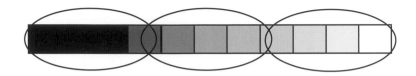

Flat space can be emphasized when the tonal range in a picture is confined to only one-third of the gray scale.

This picture, with a lack of tonal contrast, is flat.

Color Separation

The warm/cool color range must be reduced to maintain flat space. Since cool colors (green and blue) recede and warm colors (red, orange, and yellow) advance, flat space can be emphasized by reducing color to only warm or only cool colors. The concept of warm and cool will be expanded in Chapter 6, "Color."

These examples create flat space by limiting the colors to all warm or all cool.

Up/Down Position

The position of objects relative to the frame can help create flat space.

Keeping all the objects on the same frontal plane maintains flat space.

Overlap

Ideally, in flat space, objects should not overlap, because overlap suggests depth. Completely removing overlap in the creation of flat space is impossible, because every shot has a background and any object appearing in front of that background produces overlap. Overlap can be reduced with a careful arrangement and staging of objects in the frame, but its elimination is impossible.

Focus

Once any object is out of focus, it becomes flat. It doesn't matter if the object is in the FG, MG, or BG, it flattens when it becomes blurred.

Blurred objects appear flat regardless of the depth cues they contain. FG, MG, and BG objects will often blend into one flat plane when they are out of focus. Occasionally, the out-of-focus plane will read as a flat BG plane. This creates limited space, which is discussed later in this chapter.

Reversing the Depth Cues

Certain depth cues can be reversed and used to create flat space.

Tonal Separation

The depth cue of tonal separation suggests that brighter objects appear closer and darker objects appear farther away. Reversing this rule by placing brighter objects in the BG and darker objects in the FG flattens the space.

The brighter BG objects will visually advance and the darker FG objects will recede. When the FG recedes and the BG advances, the space flattens.

Color Separation

As a depth cue, warmer colors advance and cooler colors recede. Placing warmer colors in the BG and cooler colors in the FG can flatten space. The warmer colors in the BG will advance, bringing the BG plane forward, and the cooler FG colors will recede, pushing the FG into the BG. The FG and BG planes will appear to merge rather than separate.

Textural Diffusion

Normally, objects with more textural detail appear closer. If BG objects are given more textural detail, they tend to move forward or advance into the FG. FG objects that lack textural detail will tend to recede into the BG.

Size Difference

Since larger objects appear closer and smaller objects seem farther away, the depth cue can be reversed. If larger objects are placed in the BG and smaller objects in the FG, the space of the picture will flatten.

Limited Space

Limited space is a specific combination of deep and flat space cues. Limited space uses all the depth cues except two:

• Longitudinal planes. The deep space longitudinal planes are replaced with flat frontal planes.

• Object movement perpendicular to the picture plane. Movement toward or away from the camera must be reduced or eliminated. Objects should move only parallel to the picture plane.

Limited space is a challenging spatial plan to follow. Alfred Hitchcock and Ingmar Bergman used it for many of their films. This unusual type of space has a specific visual style that sets it apart from deep and flat space. Choosing a type of space for your production is discussed in Chapter 9.

These shots contain many depth cues including size change, textural diffusion, tonal and color separation, up/down position, and overlap. But convergence and perspective, the most important depth cue, is not used. Longitudinal planes normally associated with deep space have been replaced with frontal planes.

The frontal planes (FG, MG, BG) found in the limited space pictures can be seen more clearly in these diagrams. Limited space can include as few as two frontal planes or as many as three. When there are more than three frontal planes, it becomes difficult to visually separate the planes.

This picture contains only one frontal plane so the space is flat, not limited. Even though the footboard and the wall are actually on separate planes, they don't separate visually.

Limited space requires physical and visual separation between the frontal planes. There's a great difference between physical separation and visual separation. Limited space requires both. Two objects may be extremely far apart physically but when seen through a camera, they may appear close together.

In this picture there is a clear visual separation between the MG and the BG because of the depth cues.

In this version of the same shot, the BG actor and the depth cues have been removed. The BG wall is no longer visually separated from the MG. This picture is not limited, it has become flat.

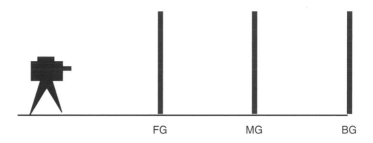

The quality of limited space is similar to looking through a series of visually well-separated FG, MG, and BG sheets of glass. If the glass sheets appear too close together, it produces flat space. If the glass sheets are visually well separated, limited space is produced.

Ambiguous Space

Ambiguous space occurs when the viewer is unable to understand the actual size or spatial relationships of objects in the picture.

Most pictures are not ambiguous. Usually pictures contain visual information that reveals the subject, the actual size of objects, and the camera's location in relation to the subject. This kind of picture creates recognizable space.

The size and spatial cues in this picture are easy to define. There is nothing confusing about this picture; it's recognizable space.

Sometimes the cues to size and space are unreliable, confusing, or disorienting. This creates ambiguous space. Ambiguous space uses any combination of flat and deep space cues. Ambiguous space can be created using the following:

Lack of movement. Sometimes objects must move before a viewer can understand the object and its surrounding space.

Objects of unknown size or shape. The actual size relationship between objects can be purposefully manipulated to trick the viewer. Size relationships between unfamiliar objects can create confusion.

Tonal and texture patterns (camouflage). Space can become impossible to define because the deep or flat space cues are disguised.

Mirrors and reflections. Multiple images can disorient the viewer, making it difficult to understand the location of objects in an environment.

Disorienting camera angles. An unusual camera angle can disguise the actual space of a picture.

Ambiguous space usually creates anxiety, tension, or confusion in an audience. Thrillers and horror films use ambiguous space to enhance their visual mood. Ambiguous space is difficult to maintain. As soon as a person or object of known size enters the picture, the audience understands the space and what was ambiguous becomes recognizable.

Comparing the Four Space Types

Any picture can be arranged using one of the four basic types of space. These drawings illustrate four ways to structure the space of a location.

The first version uses deep space. The picture still exists on a two-dimensional surface but it has an illusion of depth. There are several longitudinal planes, one-point perspective, shape change, size difference, textural diffusion, color separation, tonal separation, and up/down position. The camera will crane down and dolly right as the BG actor walks perpendicular to the picture plane.

This is flat space. The walls are frontal, and there are no longitudinal planes or converging lines. The actors are staged on the same horizontal plane; they're the same size, they have the same amount of textural detail, and any movement will be parallel to the picture plane. The camera will zoom or dolly parallel to the frontal planes.

This third version is limited space. The depth cues include size change, textural diffusion, color and tonal separation, but there are no longitudinal planes, only frontal surfaces. Eliminating longitudinal surfaces is critical to creating limited space.

The fourth version is ambiguous because the camera placement and the size and spatial relationships of the objects are misleading or confusing. The camera's physical placement is unclear. Objects may be recognizable but their relative scale and visual relationship seems incorrect. The unreliability of the spatial cues has made the space ambiguous.

Each of these four pictures brings the story to life, but each version is visually unique. What type of space is most appropriate for your production? Will deep space best visualize the ideas in your story, or will a combination of flat and deep space be necessary? Ambiguous space may be best for parts of your production because of its specific effect on the audience. Chapter 9, "Story and Visual Structure," will explain why and how to choose a particular type of space.

Controlling Space During Production

Here is a practical situation. Tomorrow you're going to direct a scene and you've decided to use deep space. How can you create deep space?

1. **Emphasize longitudinal planes**. Any wall, floor, or ceiling can create a longitudinal plane. Keep frontal planes out of the shot because they're flat. Including longitudinal planes is the most important way to create deep space.

2. **Stage objects perpendicular to the picture plane** (toward or away from the camera). This is commonly called *staging in depth*. Arrange the objects emphasizing size change. Objects in the FG should be larger and objects in the BG should be much smaller. Keep movement perpendicular to the picture plane to emphasize size change, textural diffusion change, and movement in depth.

3. **Move the camera**. Get a dolly, a crane, or hand-hold the camera but keep it moving as much as possible. Be sure to motivate the camera moves by linking them to object movement or dramatic purpose. Dollying in and out, tracking left and right, and craning up and down create relative movement.

4. **Take advantage of tonal separation**. Light scenes with more tonal contrast. Make objects in the FG brighter than objects in the BG.

5. **Use a wide angle lens**. A wide angle lens has a wider field of view and a greater ability to include more depth cues in the picture. Wide angle lenses also have a greater depth of field than other lenses. Depth of field refers to the area in front of the lens that is in acceptably sharp focus. Objects must be in focus if they're going to be used as depth cues.

Perhaps you've changed your mind and tomorrow you'll use flat space. Take advantage of the flat space cues:

1. **Eliminate perspective**. Remove all longitudinal planes and emphasize frontal planes.

2. **Stage objects parallel to the picture plane**. Keep the objects in the picture on a single, frontal plane so that they remain the same size. Keep movement parallel to the picture plane (this is sometimes called *flat staging*). If objects move perpendicular to the picture plane, use telephoto lenses to minimize the depth cues.

3. **Remove relative movement**. Don't use a dolly or crane for camera movement unless the dolly moves parallel to frontal planes. A tripod and a zoom lens may be all you need because the camera should tilt and pan only to maintain flat space. Zooming will keep the space flat but if you hate the zoom lens, don't use one.

4. **Reduce tonal/color separation**. It will be important to reduce tonal contrast and condense the gray scale. The production designer should reduce the tonal range of the set to one third of the gray scale. Color should be limited to

all warm or all cool colors. Reversing the depth cue of color and tonal separation can further enhance the flat space.

5. **Use telephoto lenses**. A longer, telephoto lens excludes depth cues because of the lens's narrow field of view. The longer lens will require objects to be staged farther away from the camera, eliminating the depth cues of size difference and textural diffusion. When objects are the same size, the picture looks flatter. Don't be fooled into thinking that a telephoto lens optically flattens the image—it can't. Using the flat space cues, not just a lens, creates flat space. See the appendix for a complete explanation of lenses and space.

6. **Let objects blur**. A shallow depth of field will allow the backgrounds to go out of focus. Blurred objects eliminate depth and emphasize flat space.

Part One of this chapter has outlined the basic types of visual space, but space is a complex visual component. Part Two will discuss the frame itself.

PART TWO: THE FRAME

Part Two explains various secondary spatial concepts that makes space more visually useful. This includes aspect ratio (defining the physical proportion of a frame), surface divisions (dividing the picture plane), and open space (creating space outside of the screen). Lastly, the Principle of Contrast & Affinity will be related to space.

Aspect Ratio

Aspect ratio is a pair of numbers indicating the size relationship between the width and height of a frame. For example, 1.5:1 is an aspect ratio. The first number, 1.5, is the width of the frame. The second number, usually 1, indicates the height of the frame. A colon (:) often separates the two numbers. The aspect ratio numbers are the width and height proportion, not the actual size of the frame.

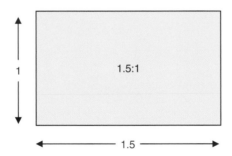

This frame has an aspect ratio of 1.5:1, which was determined by measuring the height (usually given the measurement of 1), and then comparing the height to the width. Because the width is 1½ times greater than the height the aspect ratio is 1.5:1.

The aspect ratio of a picture plane can be determined by dividing the measured height into the width. For example, a screen 20 feet high and 60 feet wide has an aspect ratio of 3.0:1. The math for this calculation is simple: 60 ÷ 20 = 3. The screen is three times wider than it is high.

The term *aspect ratio* can be applied to any type of film, video, or digital frame. This includes cameras where we capture pictures, and screens where we watch pictures.

The Film Frame Aspect Ratio

In standard 35 mm motion picture film, each 35 mm frame is four perforations high. The largest possible frame size (called *Full Aperture*) is approximately 1.33:1 or a frame that is 1⅓ times wider than it is high.

Full Aperture cameras photograph an image in this entire 1.33 area. Super 35 is another term for a Full Aperture camera. These cameras are often used to photograph special-effects shots because the picture area covers the entire frame, offers higher resolution, and allows for greater flexibility in repositioning the image during postproduction. Entire films are often shot in Super 35, which allows the final film to be released in a variety of aspect ratios.

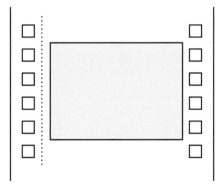

Most 35 mm film cameras photograph on a smaller 1.33 portion of the 35 mm frame called Academy Aperture. These cameras don't photograph an image on the left side of the frame because that area is used for the film's sound track (indicated by the dotted line). Films shot with Academy Aperture cameras do not have the aspect ratio flexibility available with Super 35 cameras.

The Digital Frame Aspect Ratio

Professional digital cameras used for theatrical cinema tend to mimic film camera aspect ratios. Other types of digital cameras are used for a wide variety of other media so a digital camera can use various aspect ratios as described below.

Aspect ratio also refers to the shape of the picture plane and the screen. Remember that the picture plane is the "window" within which the pictures exist. Understanding the different aspect ratios is important because the frame proportions for different screens vary. The visual planning for a television program can be completely different from a feature film. Visual content for the Internet provides the opportunity to create new or changing aspect ratios.

There are many standard aspect ratios in use for theatrical motion picture screens, television screens, and computer screens. The most common screen aspect ratio for theatrical films is 1.85:1.

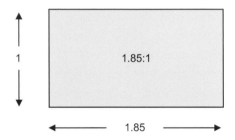

The 1.85:1 frame or screen is approximately 1⅞ times wider than it is high.

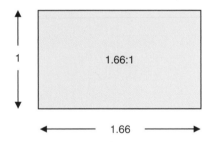

The motion picture screen aspect ratio standard in Europe is 1.66:1. The screen is 1⅔ times wider than it is high.

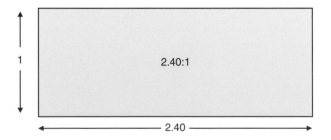

A much wider theatrical screen aspect ratio 2.40:1 is also in use. Here, the frame is almost 2½ times wider than it is high. Originally called Cinemascope, this system uses anamorphic lenses to produce this wide aspect ratio. A complete discussion of this system is included in the appendix.

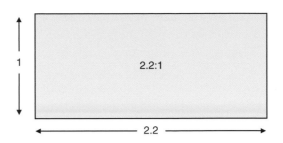

A movie can also be released in 70 mm, which has an aspect ratio of 2.2:1. More details about 70 mm are outlined in the appendix.

Imax and Omnimax, developed in the late 1960s, are two giant screen formats that use special 65 mm cameras and unique 70 mm projectors. Each frame of Imax or Omnimax is 15 perforations wide with a screen aspect ratio of approximately 1.3:1. Imax uses normal, spherical lenses and is projected on a giant, flat screen. Omnimax uses a fisheye lens and is projected on a huge, tilted, dome-shaped screen.

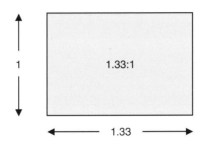

Television and computer screens have a limited range of aspect ratios. Standard NTSC television and many consumer computer screens are approximately 1.33:1.

Measuring the 1.33:1 frame or screen, the width is 1⅓ times greater than the height. Another way to describe television's aspect ratio is 4 × 3, meaning it is four "units" wide and three "units" high. Often, television's aspect ratio is described as 3 × 4, which is technically incorrect, but it still refers to the 4 × 3 aspect ratio.

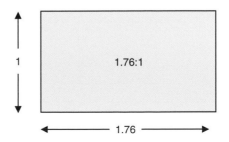

Most high-definition television (HDTV) screens have an aspect ratio of 1.76:1 or 16 × 9 (16 units wide and 9 units high).

Television shows made before 2002 were produced in the old standard NTSC 1.33:1 aspect ratio. Since then, most television production is done in the HD 1.76:1 format. This proportion is nearly compatible with standard 1.85:1 theatrical films shot after 1952 (before 1952 feature films were shot with aspect ratios of 1.66:1 and 1.33:1). Conventional 1.33 television images do not fit onto the 1.76 screen. Many HD televisions letterbox the sides of the 16 × 9 screen or distort the picture to make various aspect ratios fit or fill the 1.76:1 screen.

Aspect ratio compatibility problems occur whenever theatrical 2.40, 1.85, or 1.66 films are presented on conventional NTSC 1.33 television screens. See the Appendix for an explanation of this problem and its solutions.

Surface Divisions

The screen is a flat surface that can be divided into smaller areas using surface divisions. These divisions provide a unique tool for visual storytelling.

Dividing the Frame

There are several ways to divide the frame: halves, thirds, grids, square on a rectangle, and the Golden Section.

Halves: The simplest way to divide the frame is in the middle.

The division of the middle can be horizontal, vertical, or diagonal (the diagonal can be left to right or right to left).

Thirds: The frame can be divided into thirds.

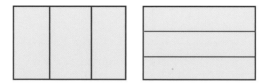

Most often, the divisions are vertical but they can also be horizontal. In painting, the vertical division of thirds is called a *triptych*.

Grids: Obviously, the frame can be divided into fourths, fifths, sixths, or more. All these divisions are grids.

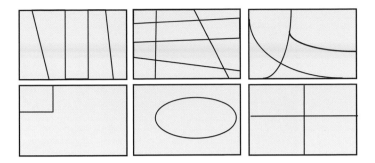

The grid encompasses a wide range of variations.

Square on a Rectangle: This is a unique surface division that occurs within any rectangular frame.

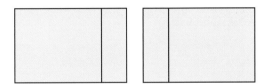

This division generates a square within the rectangular frame. The height of the square is the same as the height of the screen. The square can occur on the left or right side of the overall frame.

The Golden Section: Dividing a frame using this system is fairly complex.

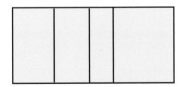

This frame has been divided using the Golden Section proportion. No two divisions will ever be the same size yet they will always relate back to the overall frame. A detailed explanation of the Golden Section is included in the appendix.

Anything that divides the frame into two or more areas is a surface division.

The divider can be an optical split screen (showing two or more separate images) as in Quentin Tarantino's *Kill Bill*. However, the divider is usually an actual object in the shot.

A division of the middle can be a doorway between two people.

Or it can be the tonal change in a BG wall.

The horizon line creates a division of the middle.

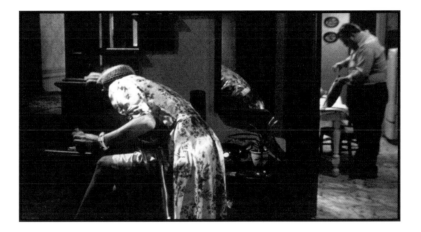

A doorway can create a square on the rectangle division.

A division of thirds can be windows.

Here, the vertical walls divide the frame into thirds.

A grid can be created by the complex architecture of a room or by patterns of light and shadows.

There are several ways surface divisions can be used to help tell a story:

1. Surface divisions can emphasize similarities and differences between objects.

 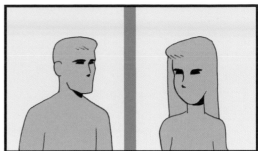

The first shot has no surface division. When a surface division is added, as in the next shot, the viewer is compelled to compare the two people. The surface division has changed one large screen into two small screens. The actual surface division can be anything: a pole, a tree, the corner of a building, a shadow, etc. The surface division asks the audience to compare and contrast each area of the divided frame.

The emotional separation between mother and son is visualized with a vertical surface division that divides the frame. The picture loses its meaning when the division is removed.

2. Surface divisions can help direct the eye to specific areas of the frame for directorial emphasis.

The full 2.40:1 frame allows the viewer's eye to wander.

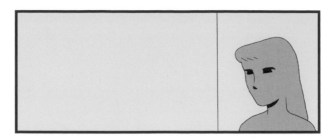

Adding a surface division places the actor in a new, smaller area of the frame. The surface division acts like a visual fence and confines the audience's attention to one portion of the frame.

Here, the grid surface division causes the viewer to concentrate on the woman and then the man in the BG. The surface division directs the viewer's attention to part of the frame and keeps it there.

3. Surface divisions can alter a picture's fixed aspect ratio. A movie or television show is limited to one aspect ratio (there are some exceptions that change aspect ratio during the film such as Able Gance's *Napoleon* (1927) and Douglas Trumbull's *Brainstorm* (1983). Changing the aspect ratio is useful because a fixed aspect ratio may get boring or is inappropriate for parts of a story.

Viewers are first confronted with the 1.33, 1.85, or 2.40 screen when they enter the theatre or sit down in front of a television or computer screen. The screen's aspect ratio won't change. Imagine an art museum where all the paintings are exactly the same size, the same shape, and in identical frames. One fixed frame is not necessarily right for every picture. Visual variety in the screen's proportion is useful. Aspects of a story can be more visual by dividing the frame into halves, thirds, girds, or squares.

In each of these pictures, a new aspect ratio has been created using a surface division. All the action will take place within the new, temporary frame.

4. Surface divisions can comment on a story situation.

The division of thirds helps to communicate the trapped feeling of the character.

The surface division of the window emphasizes the emotional separation between the two characters.

Closed and Open Space

Frame lines are the reason that most pictures are closed space.

Frame lines surround most pictures. In a magazine or book, the frame lines are the edges of the picture itself or the page. Museums display pictures in frames that create a closed border around the picture. Plastic frames enclose televisions and computer screens, and dark fabric that clearly marks the limits of the screen surrounds movie screens. The pictures exist inside the frame, not outside the frame. This is called closed space. These frame lines are so visually strong, so omnipresent, and so fixed that pictures are visually locked in or closed by the frame lines. Almost every picture we see is closed space.

The visual component of line can contribute to the closed space. Not only do the frame lines enclose the space, but the picture itself is full of horizontal and vertical lines that visually reinforce the frame lines. Exaggerating the vertical and horizontal lines reveals how much of the picture's visual construction is composed of lines that parallel the frame and emphasize the closed space. Vertical or horizontal lines are usually present in most pictures, emphasizing the closed space already created by the frame lines.

Open Space

Open space is a unique type of space that can exist outside the frame lines of the screen. It's difficult to create, but when it does occur, it pushes past the closed frame lines that surround pictures and gives the audience a sense of space outside of the frame.

A picture of a vast desert or a sky is not open space. Creating open space has nothing to do with the actual location. In fact, creating open space in a desert is difficult.

Open space occurs when the picture seems to extend past the frame lines. Of course the picture can never actually exist outside the frame (and 3D movies aren't open space). Open space occurs when something in the frame is visually powerful enough to temporarily erase the frame lines and create a sense of visual space outside the frame.

Creating open space is difficult but it can be achieved with the help of a large screen, intense movement, and the elimination of lines that keep the space closed.

Large Screens

It is easier to produce open space on a large screen. In fact, the bigger the screen, the easier it gets. Giant Imax screens can easily generate open space but large conventional movie screens in big theatres can work almost as well. As the screen size increases, the frame lines move to the edges of our peripheral vision. With giant screens like Omnimax, the frame lines may be completely out of sight so that our vision is surrounded by a picture that has no frame lines at all. As the frame lines move out of visual range, the chances of creating open space increase.

As the screen size shrinks, the chances of creating open space diminish. Television and computer screens won't produce open space because they're too small and have overwhelming frame lines. In most television viewing situations, the viewing room is full of furniture creating additional verticals and horizontals that enhance the already strong frame lines of the television itself. There's no possibility that the pictures on a television or computer screen will overpower the viewing environment, so the space will remain closed. Pictures on hand-held video devices will always be closed. A carefully controlled home theatre environment using a large screen TV might promote open space, but a movie theatre provides the best chance of creating open space because of the giant screen and the darkened environment that deemphasizes the frame lines.

Strong Visual Movement

Movement is the one visual component that is missing in frame lines so it's the most likely weapon against closed space. Movement that is visually stronger than the frame line can create open space. The screen's frame lines are solid, locked down visual anchors that enclose the picture. An extremely dynamic movement or set of movements within the picture can overwhelm the frame line and give the audience a sense that movement is occurring both within and beyond the picture frame.

There are three kinds of movement that can open the frame. One is a random, multidirectional movement of objects in the frame.

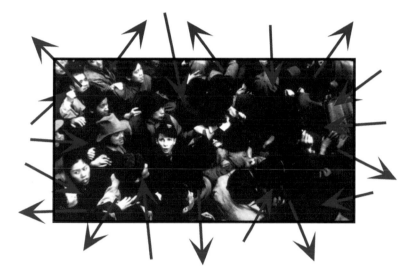

A random, multidirectional movement that fills the frame may have enough visual intensity, or dynamic, to push open the frame lines and create space beyond the actual frame. As the audience watches the screen, the movement will visually overwhelm the frame lines, and the audience will sense visual space outside of the frame.

Movement in or out of the frame can also create open space. The movement must be large in relation to the frame, slow enough to be seen by the audience, yet fast enough to generate visual intensity to overpower the frame lines.

An example of this type of open space is the opening shot of *Star Wars* (1977). When the enormous spaceship enters the top of the frame, the audience feels that it is not only on screen, but also over their heads, outside the frame, in the theatre. The ship's movement creates open space and the top frame line seems to disappear or open as the spaceship enters frame.

Open space is also created when the spaceships in *Star Wars* travel at "light speed." The sudden stretching of the stars creates movement that is more visually powerful than the frame lines. The stars seem to suddenly extend beyond the frame.

An object entering frame won't necessarily create open space because the object is usually too small in relation to the frame and moving at the wrong speed. If a moving object enters too slowly, the movement is not dynamic enough to overpower the frame lines. If the object moves fast, it passes through the frame too quickly and never gets a chance to overwhelm the frame lines and create open space.

Camera movement can also be used to create open space. Although the movement won't be multidirectional, like multiple objects in frame, random camera movement including rotations on the axis of the lens can help to open the visual space.

If the camera movement is random and of sufficient speed and agitation, everything in frame will move in opposition to the stationary frame lines. This increased visual dynamic, created by camera movement, may be enough to overpower the frame lines and open the space.

Elimination of Stationary Lines

In creating open space, any line that emphasizes the frame lines must be removed. Open space is so delicate that closed space components like stationary lines will easily overwhelm the open space and keep the frame closed.

It is difficult to imagine a shot without any stationary lines. Here is a picture of a building and a diagram showing the stationary lines it creates. Lines occur so consistently in the real world that eliminating them seems nearly impossible. Even a horizon line can keep a space from opening (which is why an open desert is rarely open space). The more stationary lines in a shot, the more closed it becomes.

Because open space is so difficult to produce, and rarely occurs, it creates an unusual spatial contrast and generates tremendous excitement and intensity for the viewer. Deep, flat, and limited spaces have no specific emotional meanings for an audience but open space is an exception. Open space will always generate extreme emotional and muscular response from the viewer. The importance of this intensity is discussed in Chapter 9, "Story and Visual Structure."

Contrast and Affinity

The various aspects of visual space can be related to the Principle of Contrast & Affinity. Remember, contrast and affinity can occur within the shot, from shot to shot, and from sequence to sequence.

Here are examples of various kinds of contrasts and affinities of space.

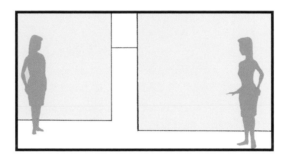

This is an example of affinity of space within the shot. A surface division divides the frame in half and both halves are flat space. Although the frame is divided, both halves are spatially similar, creating an affinity of space. The overall visual dynamic or intensity of the picture is low.

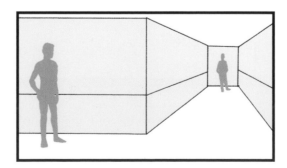

Here is an example of contrast of space within the shot. The surface division separates the deep and flat halves of the picture.

This pair of shots is an example of affinity of space from shot to shot because both are flat. These shots are low in visual intensity because of their visual affinity.

A flat shot and a deep shot illustrate contrast of space from shot to shot. The visual intensity between the two shots is high.

Contrast of space can also occur from sequence to sequence, where one group of scenes is uniformly flat and the next group is uniformly deep. Affinity from sequence to sequence occurs when all shots in a group of sequences use the same type of space.

The Principle of Contrast & Affinity can also be used with ambiguous and recognizable space, open and closed space, and surface divisions.

People often comment that deep space looks interesting and flat space looks dull. That's a generalization, which is easy to reverse, but the reaction is understandable. The viewer is responding to the contrasts found in deep space and the affinities found in flat space.

Deep space is inherently more intense than flat space. Producing deep space requires contrasts such as large and small objects, light and dark tones, warm and cool colors, and textured and textureless surfaces. Contrast creates intensity, so as a space deepens, the visual intensity increases.

Flat space can also be produced using contrasts, but it's often created with affinities, which lack visual intensity. When objects are staged on a single frontal plane, there is no contrast in size. Flat space also uses a limited tonal and color range, emphasizes textural similarities, and eliminates relative movement. The affinity used to create flat space reduces visual intensity.

Space is a large, complex visual component. When you browse through a magazine, view pictures in a museum, or watch a film, try to define the visual space in the pictures. Is it flat, deep, limited, or perhaps a combination? Learn to define the space in other work and then train yourself to control space when designing an environment or looking through the viewfinder of your camera.

Are there only four types of space? No. Deep, flat, limited, and ambiguous space offers a wide range of visual possibilities, but alternatives exist.

A scale from flat to deep reveals the available spatial variations.

Define your own visual space. Mix and match the deep and flat cues to create a space that best suits you and your story. Perhaps your new type of space uses all the depth cues but the colors are only cool. Maybe you prefer limited space but you need movement perpendicular to the picture plane. Fine. Use it. Make new visual rules that satisfy your requirements, but whatever you decide, adhere to your rules or understand what will happen if you don't.

Films to Watch

It helps to see space in use. There are brilliant examples in television commercials, music videos, computer games, television programs, and short films.

If you've never seen the following films, get the videos and watch them. The visual aspects of any film are best revealed when you view the film with the sound off (although your first viewing of any film should always be with sound). The more times you watch a film silently, the more you'll learn about its visual structure.

The wonderful aspect of studying pictures is that there are no secrets. The ingredients in food, for example, can be hidden. You eat a delicious meal but can't guess the secret recipe. A picture's visual structure can't hide because everything is visible on the screen. The more times you watch a film, the more the visual ingredients will reveal themselves.

The following films are excellent examples of well-controlled space.

Deep Space

Touch of Evil (1958)

Directed by Orson Welles

Written by Orson Welles

Photographed by Russell Metty

Art Direction by Robert Clatworthy

Watch this deep space noir classic. This film is a catalog of deep space cues and how to use them for maximum effect. Of course Welles' *Citizen Kane* is also an excellent example of extremely deep space.

Flat Space and Surface Division

Klute (1971)

Directed by Alan Pakula

Written by Andy and Dave Lewis

Photographed by Gordon Willis

Art Direction by George Jenkins

Manhattan (1979)

Directed by Woody Allen

Written by Allen and Marshall Brickman

Photographed by Gordon Willis

Production Design by Mel Bourne

Klute and *Manhattan* were both photographed by Gordon Willis. *Klute* is a solid example of consistent flat space, which creates the claustrophobic mood of the story. *Manhattan* uses flat space and surface divisions to isolate the uncommunicative characters.

Witness (1985)

Directed by Peter Weir

Written by Earle Wallace and William Kelley

Photographed by John Seale

Production Design by Stan Jolley

Witness is about the contrast between the rural Amish community (flat space) and the urban police (deep space).

American Beauty (1999)

Directed by Sam Mendes

Written by Alan Ball

Photographed by Conrad Hall

Production Design by Naomi Shohan

The visual structure in *American Beauty* is a constant, flat space. Watch for the emphasis of frontal surfaces created by walls, windows, and doorways.

Limited Space

Fanny and Alexander (1982)

Directed by Ingmar Bergman

Written by Ingmar Bergman

Photographed by Sven Nykvist

Production Design by Anna Asp

Bergman and his cinematographer Sven Nykvist are masters at using flat and limited space. It creates a unique visual world for their stories.

Ambiguous Space and Surface Divisions

Don't Look Now (1973)

Directed by Nicolas Roeg

Written by Allan Scott and Chris Bryant

Photographed by Anthony Richmond

Art Direction by Giovanni Soccol

The ambiguous space is used to create tension and confusion in the audience. The characters are swept up in a story full of mystery and questionable deception. Ambiguous space characterizes this mood.

4

Line and Shape

Lines are everywhere in the real world. For example, doorways have two vertical lines, and a volleyball has one curved line. The real world is also full of shapes. A door is a rectangle and volleyball is a sphere. Lines and shapes are closely linked because they define each other.

Line

Line differs from the other visual components, because lines appear only due to tonal or color contrast. Depending on this contrast, a line can be revealed or obscured. Lines exist in an infinite number of ways in the real world and in the screen world. To make recognizing them easier, lines can be divided into seven perceptual types: edge, contour, closure, intersection of planes, imitation through distance, axis, and track.

Edge

The apparent line around the borders of any two-dimensional object is called *edge*.

These four lines are a drawing of a piece of paper. Obviously, a piece of paper is not truly two-dimensional, but for our purposes it can be considered two-dimensional. When you look at this drawing of four lines, you imagine a piece of paper. Examine a real piece of paper, like this book page. There aren't actually any lines around the page, but the edges of the page are similar to lines. We accept this drawing of four lines as a representation of the edges of the page, but actually, a piece of paper, or any two-dimensional object, has no lines.

Lines will appear only if there is tonal or color contrast. A piece of white paper on a black background is easily seen. When the same paper is placed on a white background, the paper and its lines practically disappear. Without tonal contrast, lines don't exist.

A shadow cast onto a two-dimensional wall is an example of edge. We see an edge or line around the two-dimensional shadow, even though there's no actual line there at all.

Contour

The apparent line around the border of any three-dimensional object is called contour. Most objects in the real world are three-dimensional, having height, width, and depth. We perceive a line around these objects.

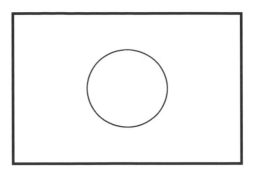

A basketball is a three-dimensional object. We accept the curved line around the ball as the border of the ball itself, but a real ball doesn't have a line around it. Our perception creates the line.

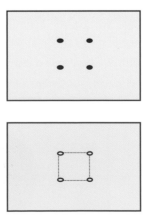

If the ball and the background are the same tone, the lines (and the ball) will disappear, because line needs tonal contrast to be seen.

Closure

Primary points of interest in a picture create imaginary lines.

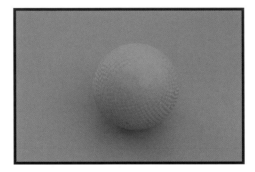

This is a drawing of four dots, but a viewer imagines lines that create a square.

The viewer connects the dots, or the primary points, in the picture to produce lines. The primary points can be important objects, colors, tones or anything that attracts the viewer's attention. The dots can connect to form any variety of curved or straight lines, triangles, squares, or other shapes.

Here, the primary points are people's heads. The closure creates a triangle and a diagonal line.

Intersection of Planes

When two planes meet or intersect, they appear to create a line.

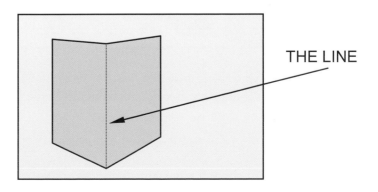

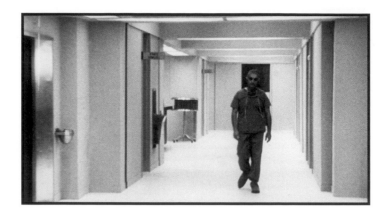

Every corner of every room can create a line if there is tonal contrast between the two planes.

If the tonal range is changed to remove the contrast between the two walls (or planes), the lines disappear. As the tonal contrast is exaggerated, the lines become more apparent.

Intersection of two planes is an extremely common way to produce lines. The corners of furniture, windows, doorways, and the intersection of walls can all create lines if there is tonal contrast between the two planes.

Imitation through distance occurs when an object appears to reduce itself to a line or lines because it's so far away.

The girders of this tower are not lines; they're large steel beams, yet at a distance, they look like lines. The same is true for the telephone poles or the distant desert road. When viewed from a distance, the objects appear thin enough to imitate a line.

Axis

Many objects have an invisible axis that runs through them, and this is perceived as a line. People, animals, and trees are examples of objects that have an axis.

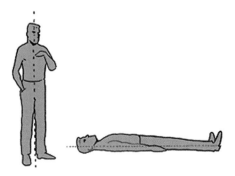

A standing person has a vertical axis. A reclining person has a horizontal axis.

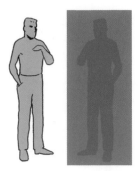

An axis, like most other types of lines, needs contrast to be seen. The axis becomes difficult to define when the tonal contrast between the object and the background is reduced.

This shot has two vertical axis lines.

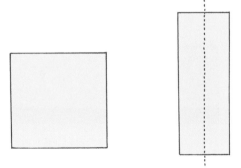

Not all objects have an axis. A square has no definite, single axis, but a rectangle does.

Track

Track is the path of a moving object. As any object moves, it will leave a track or line in its path. There are two types of tracks: actual and virtual.

Actual Tracks

When certain objects move, they actually leave a visible track or line behind them.

A skywriting airplane leaves a line of smoke behind it as it flies, and skiers moving down a snowy hillside will produce a line in the snow with their skis. The smoke and the indentations in the snow aren't actually lines, of course; they're imitation through distance or contour, creating a track left behind by the moving object.

Virtual Tracks

Most objects don't create an actual track or line when they move, but they do generate a virtual or invisible line. A virtual track is a line we must imagine.

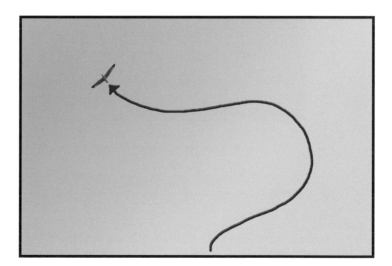

A flying bird or a moving car, for example, generates virtual tracks. The lines left behind by the bird or the car exist only in the viewer's imagination. Since tracks deal with moving objects, we'll return to line and track in Chapter 7, "Movement."

Linear Motif

Any picture can be reduced to simple lines. This is called the linear motif. A picture's linear motif can be any combination of circular, straight, vertical, horizontal, or diagonal lines.

Here's a picture and a high contrast version of it that simplifies the tonal range, and reveals the linear motif. The linear motif is found by emphasizing the tonal contrasts in the picture.

There are two ways to reduce any picture to simple tonal contrasts and reveal the linear motif. Many cinematographers use a contrast viewing glass to light their shots and check tonal contrasts. A contrast viewing glass is used like a monocle, but its glass is extremely dark, usually a dark brown or blue color. Looking through the viewing glass increases a picture's contrast and reveals the linear motif. Another way to see the linear motif is simply to squint. Squinting increases a picture's contrast, reduces detail, and emphasizes the lines that create the linear motif.

Squint at this shot. The linear motif is diagonal.

It's essential when evaluating or defining a linear motif that you analyze the line on the two-dimensional screen, not the line in real life.

In the real world, the fountain in this picture has two round bowls. In the screen world, the bowl's curved lines are not curves at all. The diagram reveals that the lines of the fountain bowl are nearly straight. The only curves in this picture are the arches.

Chapter 9 will examine the linear motif of entire films and show how important linear motif is to visual structure.

Contrast and Affinity

Line is used to produce contrast or affinity in three ways: orientation, direction, and quality. Remember that contrast and affinity can occur within the shot, from shot to shot, and from sequence to sequence.

Orientation is the angle of lines created by nonmoving or stationary objects. Most lines created by edge, imitation through distance, and the intersection of two planes are stationary lines. This includes room corners, doors, windows, furniture, sidewalks, curbs, trees, buildings, etc.

The three angles of line orientation are horizontal, vertical, and diagonal.

Linear motif is usually created by the orientation of lines. The linear motif of each picture is diagrammed in the accompanying drawing. If you can't see the linear motif created by orientation, squint at the picture to remove extraneous details that camouflage the lines.

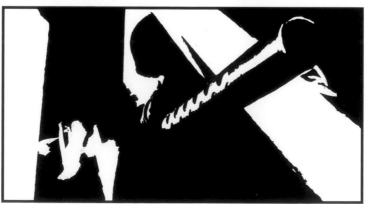

The diagonal line is the most intense, the vertical line is less intense, and the horizontal line is the least dynamic or intense line. Contrast of orientation can occur within a shot, from shot to shot, or from sequence to sequence.

This shot illustrates contrast of line orientation within the shot.

This shot illustrates affinity of orientation within the shot.

These two pictures illustrate affinity of orientation from shot to shot, because the angle of the stationary lines is the same.

These pictures illustrate contrast of orientation of line from shot to shot.

Direction refers to the angle of lines or tracks created by moving objects. In the following drawings, the arrow indicates the direction of the track made by the moving object.

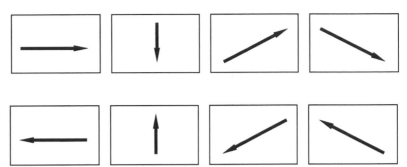

There are eight directions in which an object can move on the screen.

Affinity of direction within the shot is created when two (or more) objects move in the same direction.

In this example of contrast of direction of line within the shot, objects move in different directions.

Contrast or affinity of direction of line can also occur from shot to shot.

Quality

Quality of line refers to the linear (straight) or curvilinear (curved) nature of a line.

1	2	3	4

Lines 1 and 2 have affinity of quality of line, because they're both nearly straight. Lines 1 and 4 have contrast, because one is straight and the other curved.

Certain adjectives and emotional moods often are associated with quality of line. Most of the other basic visual components don't have preexisting emotional characteristics associated with them, but straight and curved lines often do.

Generally speaking, a straight line is associated with these characteristics: direct, aggressive, bland, honest, industrial, ordered, strong, unnatural, adult, and rigid. A curved line often is associated with these characteristics: indirect, passive, pertaining to nature, childlike, romantic, soft, organic, safe, and flexible. These characteristics can create predictable stereotypes and are only a general guide. Your own feelings about straight and curved lines will affect how you use them. Chapter 9 explains how any descriptive characteristic can be assigned to any basic visual component.

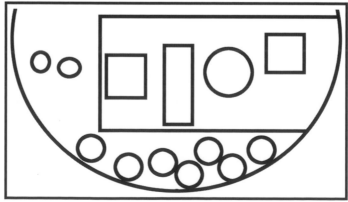

These pictures illustrate contrast or affinity of quality of line within the shot. The contrast of straight and curved lines increases the overall visual intensity. The affinity of the straight lines keeps the visual intensity low.

This pair of shots illustrates affinity of line quality. All the lines in both shots are straight.

There are many other ways to apply the Principle of Contrast & Affinity to line including thick and thin, continuous and broken, long and short, and in-focus and out-of-focus lines. These are important considerations in a drawing class, but it becomes difficult for an audience to notice these aspects of line during a story filled with moving images and sound. It is also difficult for a filmmaker to control them. Occasionally these secondary aspects of line become visually important in film and video, but usually they have little effect on contrast and affinity. Orientation, direction, and quality are visual aspects of line that are immediately useful to the picture maker, because they are quickly recognizable by an audience.

Shape

Just as there are basic types of spaces and lines, there are basic shapes. The basic shapes are the circle, square, and equilateral triangle. Shapes exist in a visual space that can be flat or deep. Therefore, shapes can be classified as two-dimensional (flat space) or three-dimensional (deep space).

The circle, square, and triangle are two-dimensional.

The sphere, cube, and three-sided pyramid are three-dimensional.

A shape can be classified as basic only if its unseen sides can be predicted correctly by examining the visible sides. A three-sided pyramid reveals all the information needed about the shape of its hidden sides. The cube does the same, and of course a sphere's shape remains identical no matter how it's turned.

Many other shapes including the cylinder and cone often are incorrectly classified as basic shapes. When viewed from below, the cylinder and cone appear identical and give no clue that one is pointed. This disqualifies them as basic shapes, because they hide their true shape identities.

Another reason why many shapes aren't classified as basic is because it makes shape recognition too complicated. Basic shape differences must be easy to see. Visually speaking, it's too difficult to notice small differences in the shapes of objects. An audience can't easily see the shape difference between a three-sided pyramid and a four-sided pyramid, for example. The circle, square, and triangle are visually different, useful, and within the perceptual reach of an audience. Simplification makes structuring the complex visual component of shape possible.

Basic Shape Recognition

The real world is filled with millions of objects, and each one seems to have its own unique shape. The basic shape of any object can be revealed by reducing it to a silhouette. Any object, no matter how apparently unique, can be categorized into one of the three basic shapes.

Here are the basic silhouettes of three cars.

The first car is based on a circle. The circle is the most benign of the basic shapes. It doesn't have an up or down or any sides. A circle has no direction or intrinsic visual dynamic. Most people describe cars with a circular shape as friendly or cute. This middle vehicle is obviously based on a square shape. It is less friendly than the circular car, but it seems to possess a visual stability and solidity that the circular car lacks. The fastest of the three cars has the shape of a triangle. It may be a high performance racecar, but its basic shape is a triangle. The triangle is the most dynamic of the three basic shapes, because it's the only shape that contains at least one diagonal line. A triangle is an arrow. It points in a particular direction, which is something the square and circle can't do.

Every object has a basic shape that can be discovered by reducing the object to its silhouette.

Faces can be categorized as basic shapes.

Trees come in three basic shapes, too.

Furniture and everything else can be classified into one of three basic shapes that can easily be seen by looking at the object's silhouette.

Light patterns and shadows can also produce circles, squares, and triangles.

The same emotional characteristics associated with curved and straight lines can be linked to round, square, and triangular shapes. Rounded shapes often are described as indirect, passive, romantic, pertaining to nature, soft, organic, childlike, safe, and flexible. Square shapes are direct, industrial, ordered, linear, unnatural, adult, and rigid. Because of their diagonal lines, triangles often are described as bold, aggressive, dynamic, angry, menacing, scary, chaotic, disorienting, and unorganized. Remember, these emotional associations are not rules and can lead to stereotypes. Chapter 9 will explain how almost any emotional characteristic can be attached to any line or shape.

Contrast and Affinity

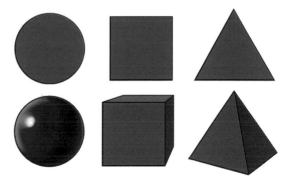

Among the two-dimensional shapes, the circle and triangle have maximum contrast. Using three-dimensional shapes, the sphere and the three-sided pyramid have maximum contrast. If the two- and three-dimensional shapes are grouped together, maximum contrast is best created by the sphere and the triangle or the circle and the three-sided pyramid. These two combinations create contrast in the basic shape, as well as in their two- or three-dimensional properties.

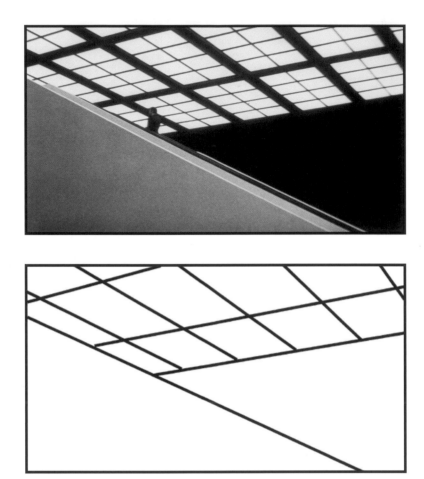

Here's an example of contrast of shape within the shot. The triangles contrast with the squares.

This picture illustrates affinity of shape within the shot. All the basic shapes in the shot are squares. Contrast and affinity of shape can also occur from shot to shot or from sequence to sequence.

Controlling Line and Shape during Production

Here is a practical situation. Tomorrow you're going to direct a scene, and you've decided to emphasize lines and shapes. How can you control them on the set?

1. **Squint**. Most lines in the modern world are vertical and horizontal because they're created by architecture. Doors, windows, and walls tend to be vertical and horizontal. The same thing often is true with furniture. What is the linear motif of the shot? Use a contrast viewing glass or learn to squint properly so recognizing the lines in your locations and pictures becomes easier.

2. **Evaluate the lighting**. Since line exists because of tonal or color contrasts, line can be controlled through lighting. As a picture gains tonal contrast, more lines will appear. Brightening or darkening an object can create or obscure lines to alter the linear motif.

3. **Stage movement carefully**. When an object moves, it creates a horizontal, vertical, or diagonal line or track. Each of these three lines communicates a different visual intensity to the audience.

4. **Create a linear motif storyboard**. Line is an important factor in planning shots. A storyboard is a series of drawings illustrating the composition of shots. But the following storyboard plots the linear motif of line orientation from shot to shot.

The linear motif will decrease or increase the visual intensity of any sequence. It doesn't matter if the sequence is a violent car chase or a quiet conversation; the contrast or affinity of line can orchestrate the intensity changes of the scene.

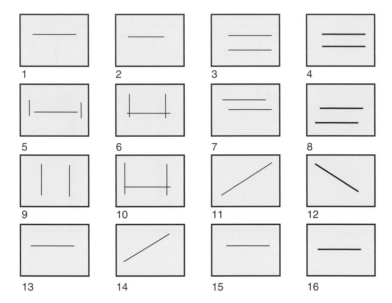

The most intense frames of this storyboard are 12-13-14, because they have the greatest visual contrast. The line orientation moves from diagonal (12) to horizontal (13) to diagonal (14). This is an extremely useful storyboard, not because of realistic drawings of people and objects, but because it uses the Principle of Contrast & Affinity to structure the linear motif of the sequence. Visually, this sequence will build in intensity toward a climax. In Chapter 9, this concept will be reviewed in relationship to a story structure.

Shape control requires careful examination of an object's silhouette:

1. **Evaluate the shapes**:
   a. **Actor**. If the actor and wardrobe are reduced to silhouettes, what is the basic shape?
   b. **Scenery**. Define the lines to discover the shapes in your picture. Horizontal and vertical lines usually create squares and rectangles. Diagonal lines create triangles.
   c. **Set dressing**. Define the basic shape of the furniture and other set dressing.

2. **Control the lighting**. Lighting can change or emphasize the basic shapes of objects in the picture. A pattern of light can create a circular, square, or triangular shape.

3. **Simplify**. Shape works best if it's easy for the audience to see similarities and differences. Use the lens choice and camera angle to emphasize, or remove lines and shapes in the shot.

Films to Watch

Linear Motif

Driving Miss Daisy (1989)

Directed by Bruce Beresford
Written by Alfred Uhry
Photographed by Peter James
Production Design by Bruno Rubeo

The house uses a horizontal and vertical motif.

Diagonal Linear Motif

Natural Born Killers (1994)

Directed by Oliver Stone
Written by Quentin Tarantino and David Veloz
Photographed by Robert Richardson
Production Design by Victor Kempster

Much of the film uses a diagonal motif to parallel the mental state of the main characters and the chaotic situation they provoke.

Shapes of Spaces

The Conformist (1969)

Directed by Bernardo Bertolucci

Written by Bernardo Bertolucci

Photographed by Vittorio Storaro

Production Design by Fernando Scarfiotti

This film emphasizes the shape of spaces. Each sequence of the film changes its use of shape.

The Shining (1980)

Directed by Stanley Kubrick

Written by Stanley Kubrick and Diane Johnson

Photographed by John Alcott

Production Design by Roy Walker

The visual style emphasizes the triangular shapes set up by the one-point perspective.

Sexy Beast (2000)

Directed by Jonathan Glazer

Written by Louis Mellis and David Scinto

Photographed by Ivan Bird

Art Direction by Jan Houllerigue

The architecture of the house and pool create the basic linear motif for most of the film. The sparse set dressing makes the architectural structure even more important.

5

Tone

Tone is the easiest visual component to explain and understand. Tone does not refer to the tone of a script (angry, happy) or sound qualities (bass, treble). Tone refers to the brightness of objects.

The range of brightness can be illustrated with a gray scale. Controlling the brightness of objects is critical when shooting in black and white or color. Working in color can distract you from the important visual control that tone has on a picture.

The tonal range of a picture can help direct the audience's attention. The brightest area will usually attract a viewer's attention first, especially if there isn't any movement. The tonal range of a picture can also affect its mood and emotional feeling. Chapter 10 discusses how to make choices appropriate for your production.

Controlling the Gray Scale

There are three ways to control the tone, or brightness, of objects in a shot: reflective control (art direction), incident control (lighting), and exposure (camera and lens adjustments).

Reflective Control (Art Direction)

The brightness range of a picture can be controlled by the actual reflectance values of objects.

These are dark tones.

These are light tones.

These are contrasty tones.

If a production requires a dark look, paint your scenery dark, wear dark-colored clothing, use only dark-colored objects, and remove all bright objects from the shot. The darkness of the pictures will be determined by the darkness of actual objects in the shot. The production will look dark, because everything photographed is dark. An actor can't wear a white shirt; it must be dark gray or black. Conversely, to create a bright look, remove all the dark objects and replace them with bright objects. To give a production a contrast look, use only very dark and very bright objects in the shots.

If reflective control of tone is going to be used for an entire production, all the lighting must be shadowless and flat. There should be the same amount of light everywhere because the gray scale will be controlled by the actual brightness value of the objects, not by lighting. This puts the tonal control in the hands of the art director and the costume designer.

The tonal range of television situation comedies and talk shows uses reflective control. This is done to solve technical problems. Since these shows use multiple cameras, the entire set is lighted evenly to give the actors freedom of movement and to accommodate any possible camera angle. The art director and the costume designer control the tonal range, or brightness, of the production. If the art director paints a set with dark colors, it appears that way on screen. Brighter costumes appear light and darker costumes appear dark. The lighting will not affect the brightness of objects in the picture.

Incident Control (Lighting)

The second method of controlling the tonal range or brightness of a picture is lighting. In this case the gray scale is controlled by the amount of light falling on objects in the picture.

A white wall can be shadowed and appear dark. The wall's brightness is now being controlled by the amount of light falling on the wall, rather than by the actual tone of the wall itself. Bright objects can be made to look dark, and dark objects can be made to look bright, depending on the lighting.

Excellent examples of incident lighting control can be seen in *film noir* movies. The term, coined by the French, means "dark film" and was first used to describe genre films of the 1940s. The tradition has continued today in films like Roman Polanski's *Chinatown* (1974) and Stephen Frears' *The Grifters* (1990). Film noir, horror, and suspense stories often emphasize incident control of the gray scale. Of course there was plenty of incident control of lighting before film noir. Silent films, photographed in black and white, depended on expressive lighting schemes to communicate the moods and emotions of the story.

This is reflective control.

This is incident control.

Here are two shots of the same scene. One uses reflective control, where the gray scale is controlled by the actual reflectance value of the objects, and the other uses incident control, where the tones are created by lighting.

Exposure

The third method of controlling the tonal range of a shot is adjusting the lens or camera. This type of control is less selective than reflective or incident. As the camera's shutter or the lens' f-stop is adjusted, the entire picture will get brighter or darker. Exposure control can't selectively make a shirt lighter or a wall darker without affecting everything else in the shot.

The tonal range of the normal exposure is given an overall shift by changing the f-stop.

This is normal exposure.

This is two stops lighter.

This is two stops darker.

Coincidence and Noncoincidence

Coincidence and noncoincidence of tone refers to the relationship between the tonal organization of the shot and the subject of the shot. Coincidence of tone occurs when the tonal range reveals the subject. Noncoincidence of tone occurs when the tonal range obscures the subject. The subject can be a face, an entire person, a group of people, or any object that is the subject of the shot. To determine if a shot is coincidence or noncoincidence, the picture maker must identify the subject.

This is coincidence of tone.

This is noncoincidence of tone.

In this case, the picture is a close-up, and the subject of the close-up is a face. In the first picture, the subject is clearly revealed by the tonal organization. The tonal scheme allows the viewer to see the face. The subject and the tonal organization coincide, so the first picture is coincidence of tone. In the second picture, the subject (the face) is not revealed. There's no light on the face, so the subject is obscured. This is noncoincidence of tone. The tonal organization of the shot hides the subject (the face) from the audience.

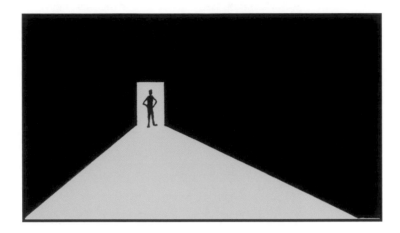

This picture is coincidence of tone. The subject is "a person." The lighting scheme coincides with the subject, and the person is revealed.

Even though the first two pictures are both silhouettes, one is coincidence and the other is noncoincidence. The actor standing in the doorway of the third picture may be in silhouette like the second, but the subject is not a face. The subject is "a person standing in the doorway." Even if the person was well lighted, the audience couldn't see the face, because the actor is too far away. This last picture is coincidence because the tonal organization clearly reveals the subject.

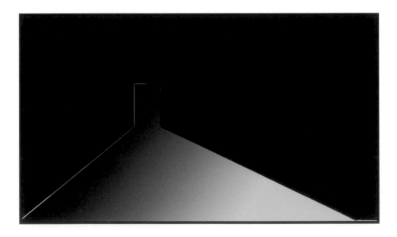

This picture is noncoincidence of tone because the person, who is still standing in the doorway, is not revealed. The subject is obscured by the tonal organization, so this shot is noncoincidence of tone.

This shot is noncoincidence due to brightness.

This shot is noncoincidence due to darkness.

Both shots are noncoincidence of tone. The subject can be obscured by any portion of the tonal scale.

Recognizing coincidence and noncoincidence of tone can be confusing, unless you have clearly identified the subject. Physically hiding the subject behind another object isn't noncoincidence of tone. The obscuring of the subject must be accomplished through the control of tone.

Films use coincidence of tone because the subject is clearly visible. The audience knows where to look because the subject is easy to see. Comedy usually uses coincidence of tone to help add clarity to the jokes. How you handle any genre and use coincidence of tone depends on your story and your personal preferences.

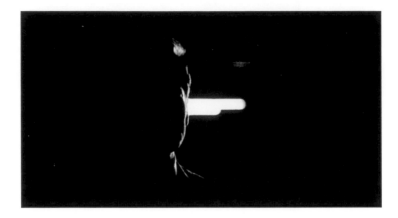

This close-up of a face is noncoincidence of tone. A key ingredient in horror, mystery, and suspense films is the audience's inability to see the subject. If the subject of the shot (the attacker, victim, witness, confidant, etc.) is hidden, it makes the audience anxious. The subject is on screen but hidden by the tonal structure.

Noncoincidence, because it hides the visual subject, often makes the audience more aware of the sound. When there is less to look at, the audience will pay more attention to dialogue, sound effects, or music.

Contrast and Affinity

Contrast and affinity of tone is easy to understand, because the gray scale organizes tone so perfectly. Remember that contrast and affinity can occur within the shot, from shot to shot, and from sequence to sequence.

Maximum contrast of tone is black and white. Maximum affinity is any two grays next to one another on the gray scale.

Tonal control must be overt if it's going to be useful. A shot designed for maximum contrast of tone must eliminate the intermediate shades of gray.

This picture illustrates contrast of tone within the shot. The tones in the shot emphasize black and white, with no middle grays at all.

Affinity of tone is difficult to achieve and maintain. It's impractical to create a series of shots using only two similar shades of gray. Limiting the tonal range of a shot or sequence to only one third of the gray scale is a more practical way to create tonal affinity. Restricting the tonal range to only the upper or lower half of the gray scale is not as effective, because a middle gray and a white or black tone can appear too contrasty.

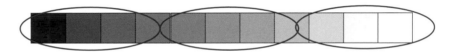

This shows the gray scale divided into thirds.

This picture condenses the tonal range into the middle third of the gray scale. The upper and lower portion of the gray scale has been reduced or eliminated. This picture illustrates affinity of tone.

Although the concept of contrast and affinity of tone is easy to understand, it is surprisingly difficult to use. Middle gray tones often creep into contrasty shots of three-dimensional objects, eroding the tonal contrast. Affinity of tone is also tricky to maintain, because darker and lighter tones are hard to remove. Color complicates our ability to evaluate tone, because it distracts our attention. Reducing or removing color makes evaluating tone much easier.

Controlling Tone in Production

If you are preparing a production, you have the chance to control the tonal range or brightness of your pictures before production begins using art direction. If you are arriving after preparation is completed, you'll have to rely on lighting for tonal control.

1. **Find the subject**. You must know where you want the audience to look. If there is no movement, they will usually watch the brightest area of the frame.

2. **Don't confuse color with tone**. You probably are shooting in color, but evaluate your lighting by ignoring the color. Shoot a black and white test photograph or watch a black and white monitor to accurately judge your lighting work.

3. **Hide or reveal objects**. Use tone to emphasize important objects and hide unimportant objects. Consider how noncoincidence of tone can be used.

Films to Watch

Contrast of Tone

T-Men (1947)

Raw Deal (1948)

Directed by Anthony Mann

Written by John Higgins

Photographed by John Alton

Art Direction by Edward Jewell

In this classic studio genre film, cameraman John Alton makes full use of lighting to control the tonal range.

Contrast and Affinity of Tone

Kill Bill (2003)

Directed by Quentin Tarantino

Written Quentin Tarantino and Uma Thurman

Photographed by Robert Richardson

Production Design by Yohei Taneda and David Wasco

The film uses a wide range of lighting styles to separate each sequence of the story.

Tonal Control Due to Reflectance or Incidence

The Conformist (1969)

Directed by Bernardo Bertolucci

Written by Bernardo Bertolucci

Photographed by Vittorio Storaro

Production Design by Fernando Scarfiotti

Each sequence of the film uses a different arrangement of the basic visual components. The tonal controls vary from coincidence to noncoincidence, and from tone being controlled by lighting to art direction.

Repulsion (1965)

Directed by Roman Polanski

Written by Roman Polanski

Photographed by Gilbert Taylor

Art Direction by Seamus Flannery

The film makes a slow progression from a tonal range being controlled by art direction to lighting. This tonal scheme parallels the emotional breakdown of the main character.

Manhattan (1979)

Directed by Woody Allen

Written by Woody Allen and Marshall Brickman

Photographed by Gordon Willis

Production Design by Mel Bourne

The visual structure has superb examples of a tonal range controlled by art direction and light.

6

Color

C olor, without a doubt, is the most misunderstood visual component. Probably due to the misguided color education we received as children, our knowledge of color and how it works is almost unusable.

Light

We use sunlight or artificial lights to illuminate objects so we can see them. Naively, we might say that sunlight is normal "white" light because it doesn't seem to change the color of objects. A white car parked outside in the sun still looks white, so sunlight is not reddish, greenish, or bluish. Sunlight appears to be normal "white" light.

By contrast, the same white car parked in a dark room illuminated with only red light appears changed. The car looks red. The red light is not "normal." But the light from the sun is not normal or white, either.

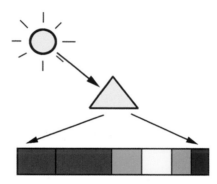

Take a glass prism and shine a beam of sunlight through it. The prism will refract the light into a rainbow, or the visible spectrum: red, orange, yellow, green, blue, and violet. The prism experiment shows that sunlight contains all the colors of the visible spectrum.

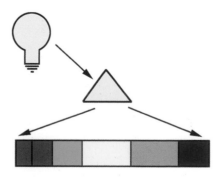

This time, the prism refracts the light from a 60-watt light bulb. The 60-watt light bulb also produces the visible spectrum but the proportions of the colors have changed. The 60-watt bulb contains more red-orange color than the sunlight.

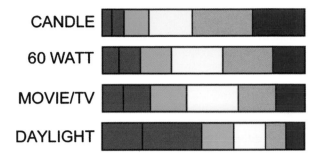

CANDLE	
60 WATT	
MOVIE/TV	
DAYLIGHT	

Here are four visible spectrums, each produced by a different light source. Each spectrum has a different proportion of color. A candle produces a reddish light; a 60-watt household lightbulb has an orange-ish light; stage lights used in color photography are less orange, and daylight is predominantly blue. Although none of these light sources produces white light, the human vision system has the ability to adjust for the color variances in different light sources and make them all appear as normal white light. For a detailed explanation of light sources and their relationship to film and color temperature, see the appendix.

Color Systems

There are two basic systems for organizing and mixing color: additive and subtractive. Although these two systems share terms and certain characteristics, each must be considered separately.

The Additive System

The additive system of color involves the mixing of colored light. Colored light is mixed by taking a light of one color and a light of another color and beaming them onto a common surface. Where the two colors of light overlap or mix, a third color is produced.

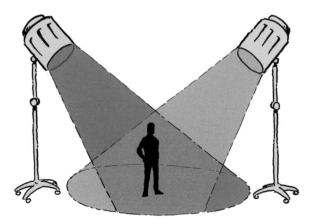

The additive system is used most often in theatrical lighting (theatre plays, music concerts, circus shows, night clubs, etc.). A red spotlight and a blue spotlight are aimed at a performer on a stage, and where the spotlights overlap a magenta color is produced. This is additive color mixing. The red light is adding its wavelengths to the blue light, and a third color, magenta, is the result.

Television and computer screens do not mix color using the additive system. See the appendix for an explanation of color mixing on computer and television monitors.

The Additive System Color Wheel

A color wheel organizes colors and shows their relationship to each other. The additive system color wheel is shown here.

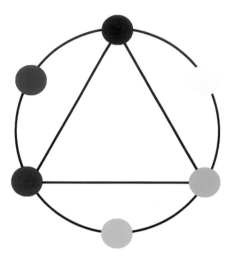

The primary colors in the additive system are red, green, and blue. Combining two primary colors produces the other colors needed to complete the color wheel. Remember, the additive system is the mixing of light.

RED + BLUE = MAGENTA

GREEN + BLUE = CYAN

RED + GREEN = YELLOW

Magenta is similar to purple, but more reddish. Cyan is like turquoise, but more greenish.

When the additive primaries are mixed together equally, they produce white light (or what appears to be white light). Colors opposite one another on the color wheel are called complementary colors. The complementary pairs in the additive system are cyan and red, green and magenta, and blue and yellow.

The Subtractive System

The subtractive color system is completely separate from the additive system, even though they share terms and certain definitions. The subtractive system is used in the mixing of pigments, which includes paint and dye. This system seems more familiar, because everyone has mixed paint in art class or repainted a room. Subtractive mixing is as easy as pouring one color of paint into another.

When red and yellow paint are mixed together the result is orange paint. The red and yellow paints subtract their wavelengths from each other and create a new color.

Almost everything in our real world has been painted, dyed, or pigmented using the subtractive system. In photography, lighting and lens filters use the subtractive system. Colors at a paint store are mixed using the subtractive system. The dyes used for fabrics and rugs; printing inks for magazines, books, and newspapers; paint for walls, cars, appliances; and colors occurring in nature all use the subtractive system.

The Subtractive System Color Wheel

The subtractive color wheel looks similar to the additive wheel but the primary colors are different, as shown here.

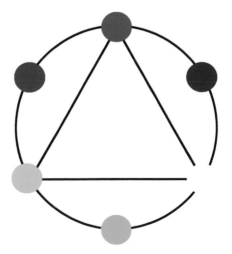

The primary colors on the subtractive color wheel are magenta, yellow, and cyan. Combining two primary colors produces the other colors needed to complete the color wheel.

MAGENTA + YELLOW = RED

YELLOW + CYAN = GREEN

CYAN + MAGENTA = BLUE

Mixing magenta, yellow, and cyan pigments together equally produces black.

Colors opposite one another on the subtractive color wheel are called complementary colors. On the subtractive wheel the complementary pairs are magenta and green, blue and yellow, and red and cyan.

Why is basic color theory so misunderstood? The additive and subtractive systems are often mistakenly combined into a single incorrect, confusing system. Most people believe that the primary colors are red, green, yellow, or blue. Many elementary school teachers believe that red, green, blue, and yellow "look" primary, so magenta and cyan colors aren't even introduced.

Another problem with teaching color is that color identification is subjective. People have different ideas in mind when describing a color. It's impossible to know exactly what someone means when they say: red, blue, or green. The variety of colors people accept as primary covers an unfortunately broad range. Additionally, manufacturing the exact paint to create a true primary color is nearly impossible, and standardization of color names is difficult, so we tend to accept a wide range of colors as primary.

Ask anyone in the business of printing pictures in magazines or books and they'll tell you that the subtractive primary colors have always been magenta, yellow, and cyan (and black to compensate for inadequacies in the printing inks). Computer ink jet and laser printers also use the subtractive system's primary colors.

Colored filters that are used on camera lenses and theatrical lights also use the subtractive system. These filters are usually colored glass or acetate sheets called *gels*. Filter colors are mixed subtractively by laying one filter over another. The mixing results are exactly the same as when mixing paint. Overlapping a cyan and a magenta filter creates a blue color. Overlapping magenta and yellow filters creates red; overlapping cyan and yellow filters creates green. If magenta, yellow, and cyan filters are overlapped together, black or no light transmission occurs. Each filter has subtracted its wavelength from the other two, leaving no light at all. How camera filters can affect the color of light is explained in the appendix.

This is not an instruction book about mixing watercolors, acrylic, or oil paints for artists. The theories and systems for mixing artist's colors vary greatly, depending on the artist's choice of paint manufacturer and style of working. The purpose of this chapter is to identify, organize, and control color in the photography of film and video productions.

The Basic Components of Color

Talking about color is difficult because words can never accurately describe a color. Commercial paint stores use names like "King's Ransom," "Liberty," or "Sorrento" to describe colors in their catalogue. Interior designers use words like "mushroom" or "peach," which may generally describe a color, but still aren't very specific. Sometimes colors are given names like "sea-calm" or "romance," which tell more about the emotion the color hopes to evoke rather than a description of the color itself.

Ultimately, it's impossible to accurately describe a color using words. What color is "candy apple red"?

Here are three red colors—any one of them could be "candy apple red."

The only way to describe a specific color is to have an actual sample of the color in hand. Commercially available systems, like the Pantone Color System and the Munsell Color System, provide color swatches that are accepted worldwide. These systems specify a color based on numbered charts or swatches of color, rather than a verbal description.

If color swatches aren't available, there are three terms that can verbally describe any color: hue, brightness, and saturation.

Hue

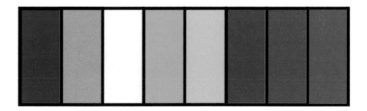

The eight hues are shown here. Hue is the position of a color on the color wheel: red, orange, yellow, green, cyan, blue, violet (or purple), and magenta. That's it. There are only eight hues. Pink, brown, turquoise, and beige are not hues. Using the hue name is a good way to begin to describe a color. Stop signs are red, a lemon is yellow, and grass is green. Although this lacks subtlety, describing exact colors using words is impossible.

Brightness

Brightness (sometimes called value) is the addition of white or black to the hue. Brightness is the position of a color in relation to the gray scale.

Adding white to a red hue creates a bright red (called pink). Adding black to a red hue produces dark red (called maroon or burgundy).

At noon, the sky is bright or light blue. At twilight, the sky is dark blue. Words can describe color only in a general way.

Saturation

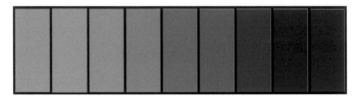

The third term used to describe a color is saturation (sometimes called chroma or intensity) and its opposite, desaturation. Saturation refers to the purity of a hue. For example, fully saturated means the hue is extremely vivid. A saturated red is a red that hasn't been contaminated by any other hue. It's 100% red.

Desaturation involves a saturated hue and its complementary color. Complementary colors are opposite one another on the color wheel.

As an example, begin with the hue of red. Like all the colors on the wheel, this red is the purest, most vivid, saturated color possible. If a small amount of cyan (red's complementary color) is added to the red hue, the red begins to change. It begins to turn gray. This is called desaturation. The more cyan that is added, the grayer the red will become. When equal amounts of cyan and red are mixed together, there will be no trace of either hue; only gray will remain. Any color will desaturate (or turn gray) by adding its complementary color. When a hue is extremely pure or vivid, it is saturated. The grayer the color becomes the more desaturated it appears.

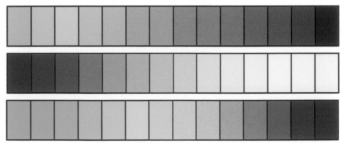

Here are the subtractive complementary pairs. As complementary colors are mixed together, they desaturate their partner and when mixed equally, create gray.

Hue, brightness, and saturation are the only terms needed to describe a color. These three terms are not exact, but using them is better than words found on designer brand paints like "sea-calm" or "liberty." To precisely describe a color, you must show a sample of it, but a color can be generally described using hue, brightness, and saturation.

There are a few other terms frequently used to describe a color. *Tint* and *pastel* mean adding white to a hue. *Shade* usually means adding the complementary color, but sometimes it means adding black. To avoid confusion, don't use these terms at all.

Look around you and try to describe the color of objects in terms of hue, brightness, and saturation. Most objects contain color, even if they appear gray. They're just partially desaturated.

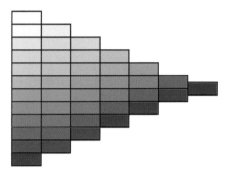

This diagram illustrates a range of colors that were created by adding black, white, or cyan to a fully saturated red. The red rectangle on the right is the most saturated. The colors desaturate as they move to the left, become brighter as they move up, and darker as they move down the diagram. Any one of the colors can be generally described in terms of hue, brightness, and saturation.

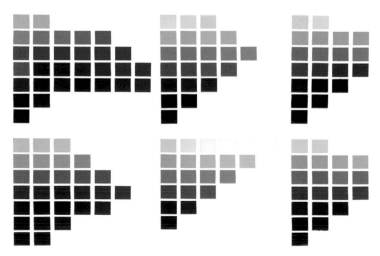

This diagram can be made for each of the six basic colors on the color wheel.

A basic color wheel always displays the hues in their fully saturated (most pure or vivid) state. But the brightness of these saturated hues is different. A black and white photograph of the subtractive wheel reveals the wide brightness range inherent in fully saturated colors.

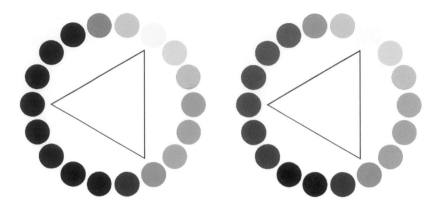

Here's a color wheel, and beside it, the same wheel reproduced in black and white. Yellow is the brightest saturated color. Orange is almost as bright. A saturated red, green, and cyan appear as middle gray. Blue and violet are the darkest saturated colors.

Knowing the inherent brightness levels of different saturated hues is important. A saturated yellow will always attract the viewer's eye first, not only because it's saturated, but also because it's very bright. A saturated blue will always appear much darker than a saturated yellow. By adding white, the brightness level of the blue can be raised to match the yellow, but the blue won't retain its saturation because it's too bright. It is impossible to create a basic color wheel where all the hues are simultaneously of equal brightness and equal saturation.

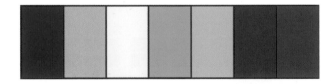

These hues are of equal saturation, but vary in brightness.

These hues vary in saturation, but are of equal brightness.

Contrast and Affinity

There are many ways to produce contrast or affinity of color. Remember contrast and affinity can occur within the shot, from shot to shot, and from sequence to sequence.

Hue

Contrast of hue occurs when the major color differences in a shot are due to hue.

The color differences in this picture are due to changes in hue.

Affinity of hue occurs when all colors in the picture are based on a single hue. Every color in the shot is green even though the brightness and saturation can vary.

Bergman's *Cries and Whispers* color scheme is based on a lightened, darkened, saturated, or desaturated red. Contrast and affinity of hue can occur within a shot, from shot to shot, and from sequence to sequence.

Brightness

Brightness refers to the tonal range of the colors in the shot. A scene that uses only very bright and very dark colors illustrates contrast of brightness. A scene that uses only bright colors will show affinity of brightness.

Here are illustrations of affinity (all dark red) and contrast (bright and dark blue) of brightness within the shot. Contrast and affinity of brightness can occur within a shot, from shot to shot, and from sequence to sequence.

Saturation

A picture using only saturated colors illustrates affinity of saturation. A picture using saturated and desaturated colors illustrates contrast of saturation.

These examples show contrast or affinity of saturation. The first example is contrast; all the color in the shot has been desaturated, except for the fully saturated red jacket. In the second example, all the colors are grayed-out, creating affinity of desaturation.

Contrast and affinity of saturation can occur within a shot, from shot to shot, and from sequence to sequence.

Warm/Cool

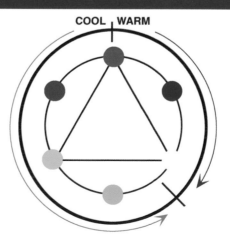

A color wheel can be used to generally classify the warm and cool hues. The warm hues are red-magenta, red, orange, and yellow. The cool hues are blue-magenta, blue, green, cyan, and yellow-green.

In terms of visual perception, magenta appears to be a combination of a warm hue (red) and a cool hue (blue), so depending on the proportion of red or blue, magenta can appear warm or cool. Yellow is a warm hue, but when mixed with a small amount of green, it appears to lose its warmth and becomes cool.

Hues can be combined in an infinite number of ways to produce warm and cool colors. Mixing complementary hues can change the warmth or coolness of any color.

Here are examples of warm and cool affinity within a shot. Contrast and affinity of warm/cool can occur within a shot, from shot to shot, or from sequence to sequence.

Extension

Color extension deals with a color's brightness and physical proportion in relation to other colors.

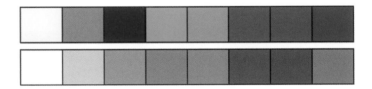

The saturated hues are shown in color and gray tones that correspond to the actual brightness of the saturated color above it. Yellow is the brightest saturated color and blue/magenta, the darkest.

Here is a picture in color, and then the same picture in black and white. Notice how the tonal range is revealed.

Don't confuse tone with color. A saturated color might look intense, but the audience's attention will probably be drawn to brightness first. A saturated yellow will always attract an audience's attention, because it is not only saturated, but also extremely bright. A saturated magenta, because it is so dark, will tend to be ignored. As any color darkens, its ability to attract the eye decreases.

Interaction of Color

In his famous color studies at Yale University, the artist Josef Albers demonstrated and defined what has come to be called color interaction.

Albers' studies clarified theories about how colors appear to change their hue, brightness, or saturation when placed next to each other. His demonstrations, based on his personal work and the work of his students, developed into a set of rules that accurately predict how colors will interact.

Making a color change its appearance requires two ingredients:

- The susceptible color—This is the color that will appear to change.

- The neighbor—This is the color or tone that will activate the change in the susceptible color.

Here are three basic rules of color interaction.

Hue and Black or White

Color interaction occurs when black or white is placed next to a color, but the results vary depending on the proportions.

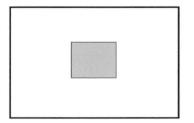 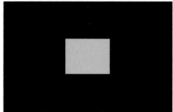

This example uses cyan as the susceptible color and black or white as the neighbor. When cyan is surrounded by white, the cyan looks darker. Surrounding the same cyan with black makes the cyan look lighter.

The susceptible color shifts in opposition to the brightness of the neighboring tone. As the proportion of the neighboring white or black increases, the susceptible hue's tone appears to shift farther away from the background tone.

If the proportions and distribution of the black or white changes in relation to the susceptible hue, the opposite result occurs. This phenomenon, known as the *Bezold Effect*, has no satisfactory explanation as it completely contradicts the usual combination of black, white, and a susceptible hue. Sometimes called the *spreading effect*, the same color appears brighter when placed around white and darker when placed around black. The susceptible color adopts the brightness of the neighboring tone.

This figure shows the Bezold Effect.

These kinds of color interactions are called simultaneous contrast because they occur within a single picture or shot.

Complementary Colors

The second type of color interaction involves complementary colors. Complementary colors are opposite one another on the color wheel. When complementary colors are placed next to one another, their saturation increases. In this example, both red and cyan are susceptible.

A red and cyan of equal proportion are placed side by side. These complementary colors will appear more saturated than if they were placed next to other colors.

As the proportion of the complementary colors changes, the larger color becomes less susceptible, and the smaller color becomes more susceptible. The red changes from a susceptible color to a neighboring color. The largest area of red is unchanged by the tiny cyan square. However, the tiny square of cyan dramatically increases in saturation, due to the large surrounding area of red.

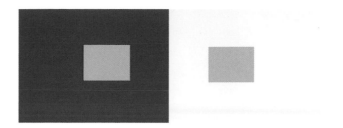

An orange swatch is placed on a blue background and on a yellow background. Even though the two orange swatches are identical, the orange on the blue background appears more saturated than the orange on the yellow background. This is called simultaneous contrast, because both susceptible orange colors are in the picture at the same time.

The same interaction can be created from shot to shot, which is called successive contrast. Now the viewer will look at one picture, and then at a second picture. This happens when an editor cuts from one shot to another. In successive contrast, only the second color is susceptible to change.

If a viewer is shown a primarily red scene and then a primarily cyan scene, the cyan becomes susceptible, and will appear far more saturated due to the color interaction of successive contrast.

Analogous Colors

Analogous colors are neighbors on the color wheel. The third rule of color interaction states that when analogous colors are placed next to one another, they appear to push apart, or separate, in their position on the color wheel.

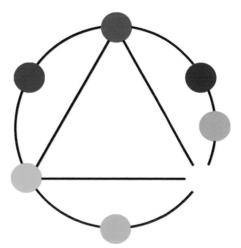

For example, red and orange are analogous colors.

In this illustration, orange is the susceptible color. An orange swatch on a red background will appear yellower. The same orange swatch on a yellow background will appear redder.

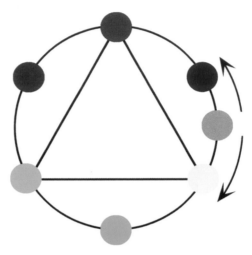

A color wheel can diagram this interaction. The red background pushes the orange toward the yellow. The yellow background pushes the orange toward the red.

How can color interaction be used in practical production? Suppose an action sequence requires red flames and, for dramatic effect, they should appear as saturated red as possible. Using interaction of color, it's possible to create a situation on screen that will help the flames appear more saturated. The solution involves simultaneous and successive contrast.

If a cyan background is placed behind the red flames, the flames will appear more saturated, because complementary colors increase saturation. This is simultaneous contrast (contrast within the shot). The red flames will appear more saturated because the viewer is simultaneously looking at complementary colors.

Another solution involves preceding the fire scene with a sequence of primarily cyan shots. This is successive contrast because the cyan color is seen first and the complementary red color follows (just like contrast from shot to shot). If the audience watches the cyan for approximately 15 seconds, and then sees the complementary red color, the red flames will appear far more saturated.

The exact physiological reasons why successive and simultaneous contrast works are not completely understood. However, a simple experiment can demonstrate the basic phenomenon.

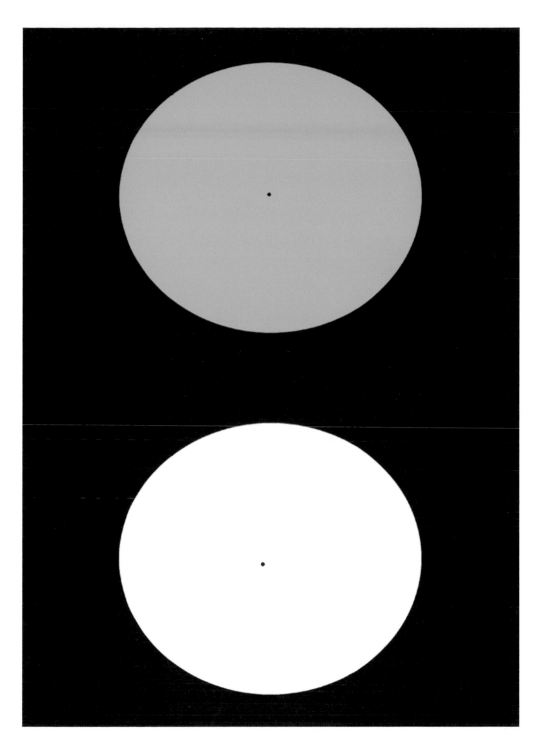

Position this book about 12 inches from your eyes in a strong light source. Get comfortable. Stare at the dot in the cyan circle for a full minute, and then shift your eyes to the dot in the white circle. You should see a red colored circle appear briefly in the white circle.

The red colored circle you saw is called an afterimage. The afterimage appears for a number of reasons. The eye will always produce the complementary color to what it sees. As you stared at the cyan circle you might have sensed that the cyan was getting less saturated, or less vivid. This was partly due to your eyes' color receptors beginning to fatigue.

At the same time, your vision system, being bombarded by a cyan color, adjusted to find a normal "white" color. Remember that human vision systems are always adjusting color and light. Since red is the complement of cyan, and mixing the two equally creates neutral gray (a visual equivalent for white), your vision system added the red color trying to make the cyan neutral gray. When your attention shifted to the white circle, you saw the red color your vision system had added to the cyan in an attempt to make it appear neutral.

When this principle is applied to the problem of the red fire, you can understand how preceding or surrounding the red with a cyan color will force the audience to generate a more saturated red color for the fire.

Color Schemes

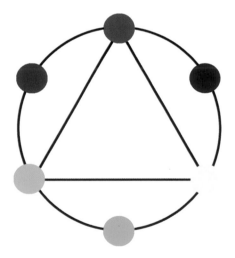

A color scheme is a color plan. Since color has so many variables, it's impossible to review all the possible color schemes, but the color wheel is a good place to begin, because it already has organized the hues into a simple circle.

Following are some possible color schemes using hue.

One Hue

A monochromatic color scheme involves finding a single hue for an entire production. Warren Beatty's *Reds* and Francis Ford Coppola's *The Godfather* use only the hue of red. Almost all the color in these films is a red hue that has been lightened, darkened, or desaturated.

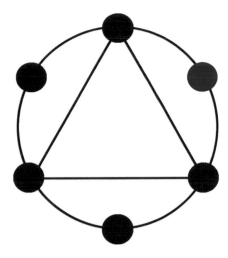

This figure shows a monochromatic red color scheme.

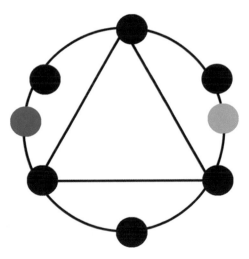

The most common complementary color scheme is blue/orange, as shown here.

A pair of complementary colors can be chosen as the basic scheme for all color in a production. The pair of hues can be assigned to any aspect of a production: one group of characters is blue, the others are orange; one location is blue, the other is orange (in Soderberg's *Traffic*, Mexico is orange and Ohio is blue); foregrounds are blue and backgrounds are orange; front light is blue and backlight is orange. Of course these arrangements can also be reversed.

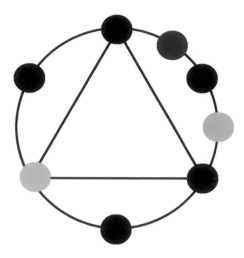

One of the complementary colors is split off into a pair of neighboring hues. This yields three hues instead of two. An example would be cyan and its split complementary orange and red-magenta. If the complementary pair is blue and yellow, a split complementary set could be blue, orange, and yellow-green.

This set of three colors can be assigned to any aspect of a production, but the three choices allow for more complex color schemes. For example, main characters can be orange, secondary characters yellow-green, and the backgrounds are blue.

Three-Way Split

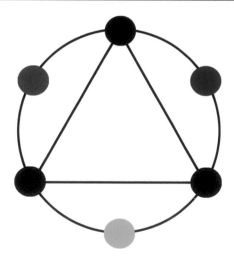

This color scheme uses any three hues, usually equidistant around the color wheel. For example, the three hue choices could be red, blue, and green. Maybe your production is a rural adventure with blue skies, green grass, and actors dressed in various red hues. Or at a forest location, assign blue to the heroes, red to the enemies, and green to the location. Perhaps night scenes are blue and green and daytime scenes are red. Here's an example of a three-way split color scheme.

Obviously, this involves four hues, usually equidistant around the color wheel. A four-way split is an extremely complex scheme.

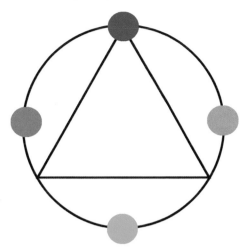

An excellent example of this scheme is Disney's animated feature *Sleeping Beauty* (1959). Magenta and green are assigned to the evil characters, and orange and blue/cyan are used for the good characters.

These schemes are based on hue only. Picking the hues is fairly simple, because there are few choices, and the color wheel organizes them so well. Next, you must decide on the brightness and saturation range of the colors in your production. This is where color can get complicated and difficult to control. At a certain point, discussing color becomes impossible, because words can't accurately describe it. A solution to the problem is a color script, which illustrates a color scheme with actual swatches.

A color script can be as simple as a group of swatches specifying the color for an entire production. More complex color scripts can show color schemes for different acts, sequences, or scenes or shots. Using actual swatches eliminates inaccurate verbal descriptions of color.

This color script simply displays the colors for an entire production. The color scheme is all cool, desaturated colors.

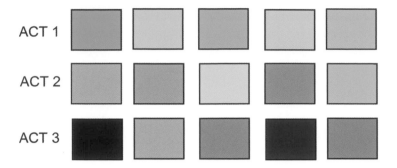

Here, the color script illustrates the color for each act of the story. Notice the contrast of warm and cool between act 2 and 3 of the story.

This color script separates the present tense from the past with two different color schemes.

This more detailed color script specifies the color range for various shots in each of four sequences of a story. Notice how the color scheme changes as the story progresses.

Don't underestimate color's value as a visual component. Audiences notice color immediately and respond to it emotionally. Animated films and computer games rely heavily on color scripts since all the color must be created. Chapter 9, "Story and Visual Structure," will look at more approaches to creating and controlling color schemes.

Control of Color in Production

There are many ways to control color: the color palette, filters, time and location, film and digital photography, and the laboratory.

Color Palette

The best way to control color is to limit the color palette itself. The palette means the actual color of the objects (sets, props, wardrobe) in the picture. If you want your finished production to appear red and desaturated, then put only desaturated red objects in front of the camera. Give yourself strict rules about the color of your production and remove colors that are wrong.

A smart production designer knows how to control color. It's not just wardrobe and wall colors. Ideally the color of every object in every shot should be carefully chosen. This can get overwhelming, so limiting the color palette keeps control simpler and allows the colors being used to have visual meaning for the audience.

The art department can manipulate the color palette. In *Peggy Sue Got Married* (1986) the vintage look of 1950 Kodachrome photos was achieved by spray painting the grass an unusually saturated green and painting sidewalks purple. In Michelangelo Antonioni's *The Red Desert* (1964), everything in a street scene, including fruits and vegetables on a cart, was painted gray.

The color scheme for *The Godfather* (1972) is basically black, white, and red. So sets, locations, costumes, and props were picked and painted with this specific scheme in mind. *Chinatown* (1974) has a color scheme based on yellow and orange (the color of dried, parched plants) with an elimination of blue, unless it is associated with water.

Audiences have a poor color memory. If a viewer is asked to remember a specific blue swatch of color, they will be unable to select that blue from a group of similar, but different, blue colors. This lack of color memory can be used to your advantage in the control of color. The hue, brightness, and saturation of an object's color can be manipulated from sequence to sequence, and the audience will be unaware of the color change. The color of objects can be changed with paint or dye in the same way that lighting changes the brightness of objects. In both cases, the viewer will be unaware of the manipulation.

159

A color often photographs differently from the way it looks in real life. This problem is called color localization. It occurs if colors change hue, brightness, or saturation when they are reproduced with film, videotape, digital capture systems, television equipment, or printing inks and dyes. The resolution of a computer or television screen will affect localization. A high-definition screen (coupled with a high-definition source) will reproduce colors more accurately than a conventional NTSC television. The manufacturing process affects the color response of various image capturing chips in digital cameras. For example, a saturated yellow flower might appear too bright, and overly saturated, when seen on a digital screen. A group of dark blue hues might appear black on film. Without testing or experience, it's impossible to determine how a color might shift.

Filters

Placing colored filters on the camera lens and the light sources can control color. This engages the subtractive system. A filter cannot add any color; it can only subtract color. A filter will always subtract its complementary color and transmit its own color.

Lens Filters

Filters can be used on camera lenses. Adding a yellow filter to the lens makes objects in the shot appear more yellow, but the filter isn't adding yellow. Actually, the filter is removing the blue color (complement of yellow) and the remaining yellow color appears more dominant.

Using colored filters on the camera lens can be tricky. A wide range of standard color filters is available for all types of photography. These filters are extremely reliable and affect the picture in specific, predictable ways. But when other types of nonstandard, colored glass or plastic filters are placed over a lens, problems can occur. The color of nonstandard filters that you evaluate with your eye may not be the color you get on film or video. A nonstandard filter that looks blue to the eye might appear magenta on film, for example. Experience or tests are the only methods of properly predicting how film or digital cameras will react to nonstandard colored filters.

Lighting Filters

Colored filters can be placed on lights. Several manufacturers provide a wide range of colored plastic sheets called gels that are available in any imaginable color.

Placing gels on lights uses the subtractive system. Whenever a gel is placed over a light, the output of the light decreases. The colored gel absorbs its complementary color and transmits its own color.

Standard gels for photography usually are calibrated in degrees Kelvin, and will accurately and predictably warm up (with an orange gel) or cool down (with a blue gel) the color of the lighting. Another group of standard gels are more selective and will remove only small amounts of one specific hue. Nonstandard gels are manufactured for theatre lighting and have no correlation to film or video camera settings at all. Although these nonstandard gels can produce spectacular colored effects, they should be carefully tested before use.

Time/Location

Color can be controlled by the time of day and the color of the location or environment.

The color of daylight changes as the sun moves across the sky. A sunrise appears more lavender, noon daylight is bluer, and a sunset is redder. Filming during "magic hour" (periods of daylight when the sun is below the horizon) produces an unusual quality of shadowless, blue daylight.

Weather conditions can affect the color of daylight. On an overcast day, the direct rays from the sun (which are more red) are held back by the clouds, making the daylight bluer.

The color of light will also change, depending on the surrounding environment. Colored objects in any location become reflectors and, depending on their size, can change the color of the light.

Photographing near red brick walls will add red to the general color of the light. In a forest, the light that filters through the trees' leaves is greener than the light coming directly from the sky.

At an exterior desert location, daylight will be reflected off the yellow/orange desert ground surface. White clouds, acting like huge reflectors, will bounce back the color, making the ambient light in a desert location an even more yellow/orange color.

Film Photography

Color can be controlled by the choice of the film stock and the method by which it is exposed. Different film stocks have different color characteristics, depending on the manufacturer and ASA. Generally, the lower the film's ASA (sensitivity to light), the more saturated the colors will appear. Some stocks look warmer or cooler, more or less saturated, have better shadow detail, or appear more contrasty. The only way to determine which film stock will be best for your project is to test it.

Color on film can also be altered through exposure. The variables here are great. Film can be under- or overexposed and then brightened or darkened at various stages of postproduction to control saturation and brightness. This book will not go into the complexities of exposure. Again, experience and actual testing are necessary to fully understand the possibilities.

Digital cameras offer exposure controls identical to film cameras, plus many more digital choices. Sophisticated digital cameras have various settings to change the look of the image. Depending on the camera manufacturer, the hue, brightness, saturation, contrast, resolution, sharpness, and exposure latitude can be programmed into the camera. This can radically affect the image recorded by the digital camera. Many photographers prefer to capture a complete, unprocessed "raw" image and then alter that image in postproduction, where even more control possibilities exist.

Laboratory

There are two types of laboratories, one for film and one for digital photography. The film laboratory uses photochemical processes involving light and chemicals that can help control the color on the film.

Flashing

Flashing means the film is exposed to light twice: once when a scene is normally photographed, and again at the lab, either before (preflashing) or after (postflashing) the photography with a camera is completed. The lab's flashing exposes the film to a precisely measured amount of light (colored or white) that will desaturate the color, lower the contrast, and, if desired, add an overall hue cast. One film camera manufacturer has added a special flashing light inside the camera body, so the flashing can occur as a shot is being photographed.

Developing

The lab can alter the length of time the film is developed in the chemical solutions. The original film is underexposed during photography and then developed for a longer period of time (called *pushing* or *force developing*) to compensate for the underexposure. Pushing the film will desaturate the color.

Laboratories are willing to experiment with filmmakers by removing or adding steps in the chemical development process to alter the color film's hue, brightness, or saturation. Some labs have special chemicals or processing steps already in place that change the look of the film's color. Cross-processing involves developing color reversal film stock in chemicals designed for negative film stock. The result is a contrasty image that super-saturates specific colors. Another lab service called *bleach bypass* adds density to darker tones and increases overall saturation. Feature films, commercials, and music videos have used these laboratory techniques to give their film a unique look.

Photochemical Timing

The lab can also "time," or color correct the film. The term *timing* refers to early 1900s lab technicians who, using clocks, would control the black and white film's image by the length of time it was left in the chemical solutions.

Modern photochemical timing uses computer-controlled additive color printing machines to color correct films. Color timing is used to correct or smooth out the continuity of brightness and hue from shot to shot. Timing can also add overall hue changes, making scenes warmer, cooler, lighter, or darker to enhance a visual style. Photochemical timing cannot target one color without affecting the entire shot.

Digital Timing

Color timing in the digital laboratory refers to the color correction of images captured on video or transferred from film to a video source. This timing is done digitally using computers, and offers far more control than is available with photochemical methods.

Color timing in the digital laboratory can independently manipulate hue, brightness, saturation, and contrast in an entire production, or any single object within one frame. Whether you're working in video or film transferred to video, digital technology allows unlimited color flexibility in postproduction.

The digital laboratory has invented the Digital Intermediate (DI), which replaces the photochemical method of color timing film. A DI is a digital duplicate of an entire production that originated on film or a digital source. Once editing is complete, a high-resolution digital copy of each frame of a production is stored in a computer. The DI allows the production team to make any type of hue, brightness, saturation, or contrast change in any part of the picture. Color timing from a DI allows for unlimited color control. The color-corrected DI can be projected using digital equipment, broadcast directly on television, or recorded back onto film and projected conventionally.

Films to Watch

Saturated Hue

Cries and Whispers (1972)

Directed by Ingmar Bergman

Written by Ingmar Bergman

Photographed by Sven Nykvist

Production Design by Marik Vos-Lundh

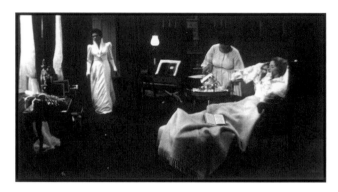

The director said that his first idea for the film was an image of three women dressed in white, standing in a red room. The entire film uses a limited color palette of red, usually an extremely saturated red.

Contrast of Hues

The English Patient (1996)

Directed by Anthony Mingella

Written by Anthony Mingella

Photographed by John Seale

Production Design by Stuart Craig

This film takes place in two locations. Red, orange, and yellow are assigned to the desert. Blues and greens are assigned to the countryside.

Punch Drunk Love (2002)

Directed by Paul Thomas Anderson

Written by Paul Thomas Anderson

Photographed by Robert Elswit

Production Design by William Arnold

The two main characters are assigned a hue that remains constant throughout the entire film. He is blue and she is red.

Affinity of Hue

Sixth Sense (1999)

Directed by M. Night Shyamalan

Written by M. Night Shyamalan

Photographed by Tak Fujimoto

Production Design by Larry Fulton

The color red is used sparingly to represent death. All the other hues are desaturated or removed from the color palette.

The Shawshank Redemption (1994)

Directed by Frank Darabont

Screenplay by Frank Darabont

Photographed by Roger Deakins

Production Design by Terrence Marsh

In this movie, blue is the color of imprisonment and red is the color of freedom.

Limited Color Palette

Sin City (2005)

Directed by Frank Miller, Robert Rodriguez, and Quentin Tarantino

Written by Frank Miller

Photographed by Robert Rodriguez

Art Direction by Steve Joyner and Jeanette Scott

Photographed entirely in front of green screens, all the backgrounds and color were created in postproduction using a computer. This technique allows for extremely specific control over all the visual components. Color is used only to accent the visuals.

7

Movement

There have been many films made without movement. Chris Marker's 1964 film *La Jette* uses only still photographs, as do many historical documentaries. But there is always movement, even in a still photograph. Movement can be created in four different ways: actual, apparent, induced, and relative.

Actual Movement

Actual movement occurs only in the real world. Almost everything in our three-dimensional world that moves is classified in this category. Walking people, flying birds, and moving cars are examples of the constant actual movement we see every day.

Apparent Movement

When one stationary object is replaced by another stationary object, the change between the two objects may be perceived as the movement of a single object. This creates apparent movement.

Film and video rely on this principle. When real world actual movement is photographed onto film or video, it's transformed into a series of still pictures. Film and video can play back these still pictures at 24 or 30 fps (frames per second), and the pictures appear to move, but the movement is apparent, not actual. To prove it, we can "freeze frame" or "step" through the film/video frames and see each still picture individually. Animation is made up of a series of individual drawings or pictures which, when shown at 24 or 30 fps, appear to move.

Apparent movement also occurs in the real world. Rows of lightbulbs on outdoor signs can blink in a specific sequence. When the rate of blinking is fast enough, the lights seems to "chase" or move along the row of bulbs.

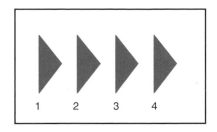

A series of stationary neon arrows on a lighted sign can give the appearance of a single moving arrow. If each arrow is lit for a short time in rapid succession (indicated by the numbers 1 through 4), the arrow appears to move.

The movement is apparent, because there's no actual movement at all, only a series of rapidly changing stationary pictures.

Induced Movement

Induced movement occurs when a moving object transfers its movement to a nearby stationary object. The stationary object then appears to move and the moving object appears stationary.

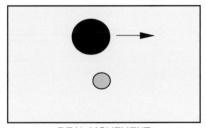

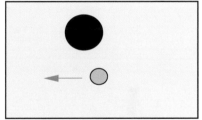

REAL MOVEMENT   INDUCED MOVEMENT

The black circle is moving to the right, but, under certain conditions, the green circle will appear to move left. Usually the movement will transfer to the smaller and brighter object.

Moving clouds over a stationary moon is a good example of induced movement. If the cloud speed is correct, the moon will appear to move and the clouds will appear stationary. The moon appears to move in the opposite direction of the cloud's actual movement.

Induced movement sometimes occurs at a traffic intersection. Imagine you are in a car stopped next to a large bus. If the bus slowly moves forward, you may feel as if your car is drifting backward. You're not really moving, but the forward movement of the bus induces the sense of movement in your car, and you feel that you are moving in the opposite direction from the bus.

Relative Movement

Relative movement occurs when the movement of one object can be gauged by its changing position relative to a second, stationary object.

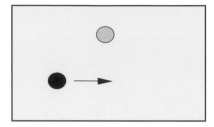 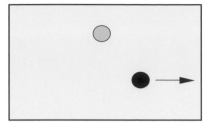

The black circle appears to move because its position changes relative to the stationary green circle and the frame.

In the screen world, visual movement can be produced only when an object moves in relation to the frame line. When objects do not move in relation to the frame line, there's no movement.

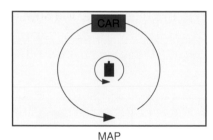 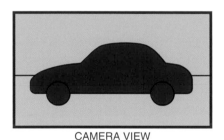

MAP   CAMERA VIEW

Photograph a moving car in the open desert. The desert provides a visually sparse environment with only a horizon line. The map shows that the car will drive in circles around the camera, and the camera will pan with the car, keeping it centered in the frame. The result will be that the car appears stationary in relation to the frame. Visually, there is no car movement, because the physical relationship between the car and the frame does not change. There is no relative movement, because there is nothing in frame to reveal the car's movement.

A very different visual situation occurs when the location is changed.

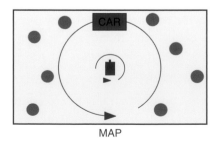 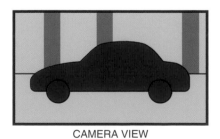

MAP   CAMERA VIEW

In a forest location, the car will drive in the same circle around the camera. As the camera pans to follow the car, trees in the background will move in the opposite direction of the camera pan. The tree movement will reveal the car is moving, even though the car is not moving in relation to the frame. The moving trees generate apparent movement, and the viewer transfers that movement to the car. There is still no relative movement because the car remains stationary in relation to the frame.

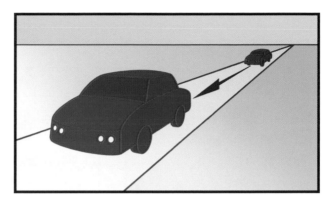

A third location is an open road. This time, the car will drive through the frame and the camera will remain stationary. There will be no camera movement. Now the car creates relative movement because its position is changing in relation to the frame. The car will move through the frame from upper right to lower left.

Simple and Complex Movement

In the real world, actual movement occurs in two and three dimensions. But the surface of the screen is only two-dimensional, so objects in the screen world actually can move in only two dimensions. There is no real movement in depth on a screen, because the screen is flat.

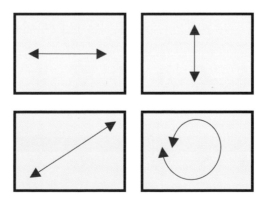

In the screen world there are only a few two-dimensional directions in which an object can move: horizontal, vertical, diagonal, or circular. These are called the simple moves.

Objects in the real world can move in depth, advancing or receding from the camera when photographed. On screen, these objects can appear to move in depth toward or away from the viewer, but it's illusory depth. Nothing can move in depth on the screen, because the screen is flat. Object movement that appears to move in depth on a flat screen is called complex movement, because it combines several simple moves onto a single moving object.

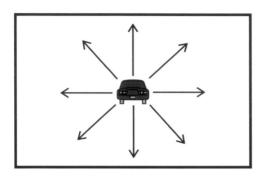 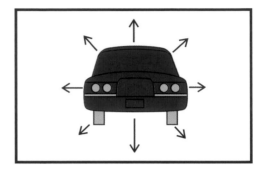

In the real world, a car can actually move in three dimensions and drive toward the camera. In the screen world the car can't move toward the viewer, because the screen is flat. The car's screen movement appears deep, because the simple moves are combined. The top of the car is moving up, the bottom is moving down, the left side is moving left, and the right side is moving right. The more simple moves combined on a single object, the more complex or deep the movement will appear on screen. The screen car also uses the depth cues of size change, textural diffusion, and speed change to create the illusion of three-dimensional movement.

Movement in the Screen World

In the screen world, there are only three things that can move:

- An object
- The camera
- The audience's point-of-attention as they watch the screen

Object Movement

Anything that moves in relation to the frame line is a moving object. Every moving object generates a track. A track is the path of a moving object. There are two types of tracks: actual and virtual. These are discussed in detail in Chapter 4, "Line and Shape." Based on the track of a moving object, there are four ways to categorize movement of an object: direction, quality, scale, and speed.

Direction

An object can actually move in a limited number of directions on a screen, because the screen is only two-dimensional. Remember, object movement can be seen only when the object moves in relation to the frame line.

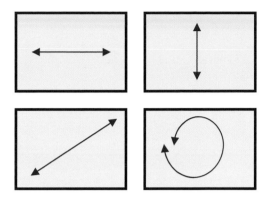

An object can make a horizontal, vertical, diagonal, or circular move. Even when an object on the screen appears to move in three dimensions, all the actual movement is only on the screen surface.

Quality

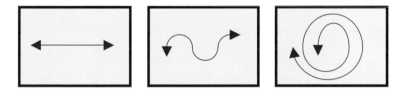

The movement of an object can be straight or curved. Since moving objects generate a track or line, the same adjectives and emotional responses associated with straight and curved lines can be assigned to straight and curved movement.

Generally, the track created by straight linear movement is associated with these characteristics: direct, aggressive, conservative, ordered, unnatural, and rigid. Tracks created by curved movement can be associated with these characteristics: indirect, passive, confused, pertaining to nature, childlike, romantic, soft, safe, nonlinear, and flexible. These characteristics can create predictable stereotypes, and are only a general guide. Your own feelings about straight and curved lines created by tracks will affect how you use them

In *Election* (1998), director Alexander Payne gave his actors specific instructions for their walking movement. Sally (Reese Witherspoon) walked in direct, straight lines, and Tom (Matthew Broderick) walked in curves.

Scale

Scale refers to the distance an object moves on screen.

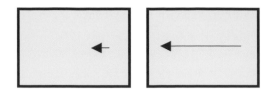

An object can travel a short distance or a longer distance in relation to the frame.

Speed

A moving object will have a rate of speed: fast, medium, or slow, for example. A viewer will judge the object's speed relative to the frame.

Camera Movement

Although an audience sees camera movement only by its effect on the objects in frame, there are three basic ways to classify camera movement: direction, scale, and speed.

Direction

A camera can move in two or three dimensions. The two-dimensional camera moves are the pan, tilt, and zoom. The three-dimensional camera moves are the dolly, track, and crane.

The audience perceives the camera movement, because it is transferred to the objects in the shot. The objects will move in the opposite direction of the camera move. When the camera pans right, all objects in the picture will move to the left. A tilt up causes objects in frame to move downward.

The same thing happens with three-dimensional camera moves. A track to the left will make objects in frame move to the right and a crane up will make objects move down. Because of this transfer of movement, camera movement itself is not as important as the effect the movement has on objects in frame.

Scale

Scale refers to a camera move's length of travel. It can move a short distance or a long distance.

Speed

A camera movement can occur at slow, medium, or fast speeds. Generally speaking, a slower camera move creates affinity, because changes in the visual components occur slowly. Faster camera moves can generate visual intensity, because the quickly moving camera view can produce rapid, contrasting changes in the visual components.

Distinct visual differences occur in the speed of FG, MG, and BG objects during two- and three-dimensional camera moves. Remember that camera movement transfers its movement to objects in front of the camera.

In a pan, tilt, or zoom (two-dimensional moves) all objects in the frame move at the same rate of speed. There is no relative movement. When the camera pans to the right, FG, MG, and BG objects will move in unison to the left. Tilting down will cause all objects in frame to move upward at the same speed. A zoom in or out will create identical complex moves on all objects in the frame.

Three-dimensional camera moves add relative movement. In a tracking shot, FG objects will move faster than BG objects. The same is true for a crane shot or a dolly in/out. A complete description of relative movement can be found in Chapter 3.

A three-dimensional camera move will always appear more intense than its two-dimensional counterpart. Due to the differences in FG, MG, and BG object movement created by relative movement, the visual intensity will be greater.

Point-of-Attention Movement

The third type of movement, point-of-attention, refers to the audience's eye movement as they look at different areas of the screen. Human vision can concentrate on only one small area of the visual field at a time. Although we have peripheral vision, which enables us to see a wide field of view, we can focus our attention on only one small area of a picture. When you look at a crowd of people, you must shift your attention from face to face to recognize specific people. It's impossible to concentrate on two faces at once.

The same thing happens when we look at a screen. Although an audience is aware of the entire picture, they can focus their attention on only one small area of the screen at a time. This is fortunate because it means picture makers can predict and control what part of the picture the audience is watching.

Where does the audience want to look in any picture? What attracts the audience's eye? Movement is first. The viewer's attention will always be drawn to a moving object. Brightness is second. If there is no movement, the viewer's point-of-attention will be drawn to the brightest area in the frame. If a moving object also happens to be the brightest area of the frame, the viewer will notice that object even quicker. When the audience is looking at an actor's face, their point-of-attention will usually be drawn to the eyes. Any on-screen vanishing point will attract the viewer's attention. An audience's point-of-attention will also be drawn to contrasts or differences in any of the visual components.

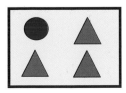 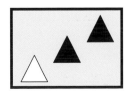 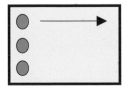

In each picture, the viewer's eye is drawn to the object with visual component contrast.

The subcomponents for point-of-attention are similar to the subcomponents for object and camera movement:

Direction

As the audience moves their point-of-attention around the frame, their eye movement creates a track. Remember, track is the path of a moving object, and here, the moving object is the audience's point-of-attention.

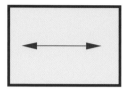 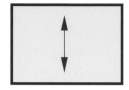 

Since the screen is flat, there are only three directions point-of-attention can move. As usual, the choices are horizontal, vertical, and diagonal.

Quality

If the audience is watching a moving object that generates a curved line, their eye movement will curve. If the movement they're watching is linear, their point-of-attention will generate straight lines. As the audience moves their point-of-attention between stationary objects, they will take the shortest path so their eye movement will usually create straight lines.

Scale

Scale refers to the distance the audience's point-of-attention travels in relation to the frame line.

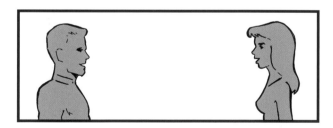

The viewer's eye will travel the entire width of the screen as it watches the two faces.

Now, the travel distance is short. Later in this chapter, we'll discuss continuum of movement, where the scale of the audience's eye movement is critical.

Contrast and Affinity

Since objects, the camera, and the audience's point-of-attention create movement, there are many ways to employ contrast or affinity. Remember, contrast and affinity can occur within a shot, from shot to shot, and from sequence to sequence.

Movement of a Single Object

A moving object generates a line. This line, called a track, can be actual or virtual. See Chapter 4 for a complete description of lines and tracks. The visual intensity of an object's movement can be determined by analyzing the track.

Movement/No Movement

The greatest contrast to object movement is no movement at all. It is possible to stage an entire production without object movement. This is sometimes called tableau staging, where object movement is minimized in favor of the stationary arrangement of the objects in the frame. Usually, however, objects move with direction, quality, scale, and speed.

Direction

  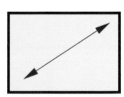

A horizontally moving object creates a horizontal line or track. The horizontal line is the least intense line. Therefore a horizontal movement has a low visual intensity. A vertical movement, creating a vertical track, has more intensity, and a diagonal movement (in any direction) is the most intense.

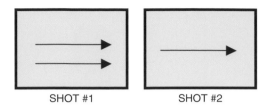

SHOT #1   SHOT #2

Shot #1 is an example of affinity of direction of track (movement) within the shot. There are two separate objects moving in the same direction. Shots #1 and #2 illustrate affinity of direction of movement from shot to shot. Their affinity of movement keeps the visual intensity low.

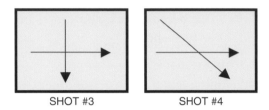

SHOT #3   SHOT #4

Shot #3 is an example of contrast of direction of track within the shot. Even though the diagonal is most intense, it's the vertical track that contrasts most with the horizontal track. Shot #4 illustrates how the diagonal track has too much directional affinity with the horizontal track to be more intense than the vertical.

Quality

Object movement can generate straight or curved tracks.

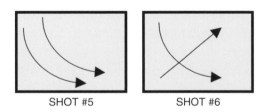

SHOT #5   SHOT #6

Shot #5 illustrates affinity of quality of movement within the shot, and shot #6 illustrates contrast within the shot. Shot #6 uses contrast of track quality (curved and straight lines created by a moving object) so it is more intense than shot #5.

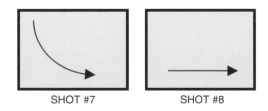

SHOT #7   SHOT #8

Shots #7 and #8 illustrate contrast of quality of movement from shot to shot. One movement is curved and the other is straight. Both shots show an object that moves from left to right but one track is curved and the other is a straight line. This contrast of quality of track produces visual contrast. It would gain more intensity if it combined contrast of quality and direction.

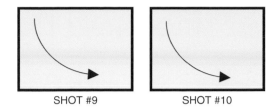

SHOT #9   SHOT #10

Shots #9 and #10 illustrate affinity of quality of object movement. The visual intensity is low because the object moves in the same direction and with the same curve in both shots.

Speed

A moving object has a slow, medium, or fast speed. If all objects move at the same speed, affinity is produced and the intensity is low. If one object moves at a different speed than other objects, contrast is created, which generates visual intensity.

Movement of an Object with a Background

The relationship between the line generated by a single moving object and the linear motif of a BG creates visual intensity. Remember, linear motif is the shot reduced to its basic lines. See Chapter 4, "Line and Shape," for a complete explanation of linear motif.

There are three visual factors to consider when a moving object is combined with a BG. The first factor is the direction of the line or track created by the moving object. Second is the orientation or angle of the BG's linear motif. The third factor to consider is the contrast or affinity created by combining the FG object track and the BG linear motif.

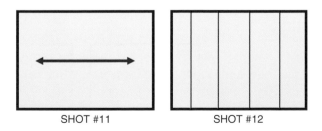

SHOT #11   SHOT #12

The arrow represents the FG moving object, and the parallel lines are the BG linear motif. When a moving object and a BG are combined, a visual relationship is immediately created, based on the Principle of Contrast & Affinity.

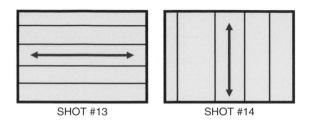

SHOT #13   SHOT #14

The least visually intense pairing of FG object track and BG linear motif is illustrated in Shot #13. A horizontally moving object and a horizontal BG motif have maximum affinity. Horizontal lines are inherently the least intense, so parallel horizontals are the least dynamic combination. More dynamic, but still low in intensity, is Shot #14, where the object moves parallel to the vertical BG linear motif.

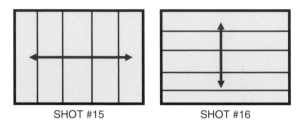

SHOT #15   SHOT #16

Shots #15 and #16 have greater visual dynamic. The contrast between the BG linear motif and the track of the FG moving object creates more visual intensity.

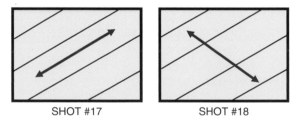

SHOT #17   SHOT #18

Shot #17 creates even more intensity because it uses diagonals. Even though there's affinity between the FG object movement and the BG diagonal linear motif, the intensity is high because the diagonal is inherently so intense. Shot #18 has the most intensity because it uses opposing diagonal lines. The picture exploits the intensity inherent in diagonal lines, and the perpendicular angles of the FG object movement and the BG linear motif.

These diagrams are only a general guide to the complex interactions that can occur between the FG track and BG linear motif. The actual subject, speed, size, tone, and color of the FG object and the BG can alter the affinity or contrast of the visual relationship.

Camera Movement

Movement of the camera can be used to increase or reduce the visual intensity. Remember, contrast and affinity can occur within a shot, from shot to shot, or from sequence to sequence.

Movement/No Movement

The greatest contrast to camera movement is no movement at all. An entire production can be photographed with only a stationary camera, or at the other extreme, a constantly moving camera. Another approach would use camera movement for only one shot. That one camera move will produce visual contrast and intensity. In the same way, if the camera is constantly moving and stops for only one shot, visual contrast will also be created, although the intensity will not be as significant.

2D/3D Moves

Camera movement choices can be limited to two-dimensional (pan, tilt, zoom) or three-dimensional (dolly, track, crane) moves. The difference between them is visually significant. Two-dimensional moves prevent relative moment from occurring, and three-dimensional moves generate relative movement.

Pan/Track

A pan creates more visual affinity than a tracking move. This is due to the three-dimensional relative movement created by the tracking of the camera. Placing FG objects as close to the camera as possible and BG objects very far away increases the relative movement. Relative movement is discussed in detail in Chapter 3.

Tilt/Crane

The tilt is usually less intense. The crane shot, depending on the FG and BG object placement, will be more intense because it creates relative movement.

Zoom/Dolly

A zoom lens enlarges or shrinks all objects in frame at exactly the same rate. There is no relative size or speed changes between FG and BG objects in a zoom shot. A zoom usually creates less visual intensity than a dolly in or out. A dolly, especially with a wide lens, produces more visual intensity, because it generates changes in the relative size and speed of objects.

There is one exception to this rule: a *snap zoom*, which is an extremely rapid zoom in or out. A snap zoom will add visual intensity, because it produces sudden contrasts in size and movement speed that are difficult to achieve with conventional camera movement.

Level/Unlevel

A tripod- or dolly-mounted camera will have more affinity when compared to a hand-held camera.

A tripod or dolly holds the camera level to the horizon, keeping vertical and horizontal lines in the picture parallel to the frame lines. An unlevel, or off-axis camera, shifts these lines into diagonals. Diagonal lines are always more intense than horizontal or vertical lines.

A hand-held camera, being used without the aid of special harnesses or leveling devices, creates additional movement as the camera operator struggles to hold the camera level, or struggles to hold the camera unlevel. A constantly shifting movement from level to unlevel translates into an increase in visual intensity or dynamic.

A moving axis rotation has even more dynamic, because all the lines in a shot will spin on axis. The greater the amount of spin, the more intense the visual contrast when compared to a level camera.

Scale of Movement

Generally speaking, the larger the camera move, the greater the visual intensity, and the smaller the camera move, the less the visual intensity.

Frames per Second Speed

The speed of a movement can be manipulated by changing the speed of the camera. This is called over-cranking (slow motion) or under-cranking (fast motion).

A projector (film or digital) always runs at a standard speed of 24 fps (frames per second). When the camera is run at its standard speed of 24 fps, the movement recorded by the camera will look normal when projected. An identical situation occurs in video when both camera recorders and playback systems normally run at 30 fps (technically the speed is 29.9 fps).

Slow motion images are created when the camera runs faster than 24 fps (over-cranking). If the camera is run at 48 fps and projected at 24 fps, the photographed action will take twice as long to view. The 48 pictures photographed each second are being projected at 24 per second, so it will take two seconds to play back what occurred in one second. This produces slow motion. There are cameras that run at hundreds, even thousands, of frames per second, which can extend a one-second event for several minutes when projected.

Sped-up movement is created when the camera runs slower than 24 fps (under-cranking). If the camera is run at only 12 fps, the 24 fps projector will run the pictures twice as fast, so the movement speed doubles. For action sequences in films, cameras often are run at 22 fps, which speeds up the movement, making stunts look more dangerous. The audience is unaware of the camera's speed change, but does notice the enhanced intensity of the action.

The extreme example of under-cranking is time-lapse photography. Objects that move imperceptibly slowly, like a flower blooming, can be sped up to condense weeks of growth in just a few seconds of screen time. A building construction lasting a year can be condensed into 15 seconds, by photographing one frame per day and then projecting the footage normally (365 frames projected at 24 fps will run about 15 seconds).

Fast or slow motion photography can be used for various effects in storytelling. Events that happen too quickly (like an action sequence) can be seen more clearly when the speed of the event is slowed down. In *The Matrix* films (1999–2003), slow motion extends time to reveal how a character moves during action sequences. In *The Untouchables* (1987), several simultaneous actions, taking only a few seconds in real time, are photographed in slow motion, allowing the audience to see how the events affect each other. Speed changes can also suggest moving from real time into a dream or mental time. In the remake of *Father of the Bride* (1991), slow motion often is used when the father daydreams about his daughter.

Action can also be sped up. Richard Lester's under-cranking camera in A *Hard Day's Night* (1964), adds energy and humor to his story, Stanley Kubrick speeds up a sex scene in A *Clockwork Orange* (1971) to comment on its impersonal nature. In the nonverbal movie *Koyaanisqatsi* (1983), time-lapse photography is used to create a surreal introspective view of civilization.

Continuum of Movement

The Principle of Contrast & Affinity can be used with continuum of movement, allowing control of the visual intensity generated by the audience's eye movement as they watch the screen. Like any visual component, affinity of continuum decreases the visual intensity, and contrast of continuum increases visual intensity. Continuum of movement occurs within the shot and from shot to shot.

Using contrast of continuum of movement requires knowing what area of the screen the audience is watching, or their point-of-attention. The visual components that will attract the audience's attention are:

- Movement
- The brightest object
- The most saturated color
- The actors' eyes
- The object with the most visual component contrast

To indicate what area or quadrant of the frame the audience is watching, a nine-area grid can be drawn over the screen or frame.

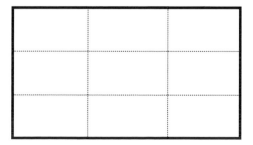

This is called a Continuum Grid.

1	2	3
4	5	6
7	8	9

For reference, the quadrants are numbered 1 through 9.

Continuum of movement is less critical on a small screen. Hand-held digital devices have tiny screens measuring only an inch or two, so continuum of movement is barely an active visual component on these screens. Since the average television or computer screen is only 21 inches, the physical range available for contrast of continuum is limited. Home theatre screen televisions provide a greater opportunity for using continuum of movement, but theatre screens and giant formats like Imax (with screens in the hundred foot range) use contrast and affinity of continuum of movement to greatly affect visual structure.

Continuum of movement deals with two concepts:

• How the viewer's point-of-attention moves within a shot

• How the viewer's point-of-attention moves from shot to shot

Continuum within the Shot

Affinity of continuum within a shot can be created without any camera or object movement.

 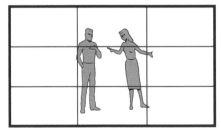

Here are two people engaged in a conversation. As the dialogue alternates between them, the audience's point-of-attention will shift from one person to the other. The continuum grid superimposed over the frame shows that both people are in the same quadrant. This means that during the conversation, the audience's point-of-attention will remain in only one quadrant of the continuum grid. This creates affinity of continuum of movement.

Contrast of continuum of movement can also exist within a shot.

The same two people are now further apart. Contrast of continuum of movement is created, because the viewer's point-of-attention must shift between quadrants Q3 to Q6 as the two people talk. The audience's point-of-attention is not visually guided by a moving object from person to person (affinity of continuum), so the audience must abruptly move their point-of-attention each time the conversation changes speakers.

As the distance between the two people increases, the contrast of continuum increases. In this widescreen frame, the audience must shift their point-of-attention a greater distance. As the screen size shrinks, the range of contrast or continuum decreases. Small and micro-sized screens eliminate contrast of continuum as a visual component choice.

Contrast and affinity of continuum of movement within a shot can also occur using object movement.

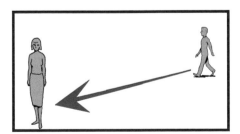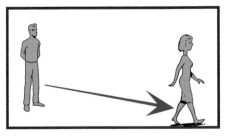

Affinity of continuum occurs when the moving objects hold and lead the viewer's attention. A man enters frame and walks to a waiting woman. The man stops next to the woman and after a moment the woman walks away.

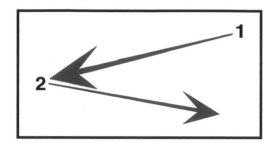

The audience's point-of-attention is smoothly transferred from the first to the second object, because the second object begins moving in the same quadrant where the first object stopped. This affinity of continuum moves the audience's point-of-attention across the screen in a choreographed pattern, following the first, then the second object.

Ernst Lubitsch's *Ninotchka* (1939) and the long continuous takes in many Martin Scorsese films like *Raging Bull*, *Goodfellas*, and *Casino* take advantage of affinity of continuum of movement in the staging of complex scenes.

Contrast of continuum using moving objects can also occur within a shot.

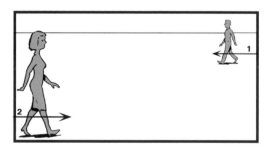

In this example, there are two moving objects. The man in the BG enters and stops. Then, after a moment, the woman in the FG enters the frame. The audience's point-of-attention will shift, moving diagonally, from the man to the woman. There is no on-screen movement to guide the viewer's point-of-attention from the first object to the second object. This change of quadrant is contrast of continuum of movement.

Continuum from Shot to Shot

Continuum of movement becomes even more important when shots are edited together.

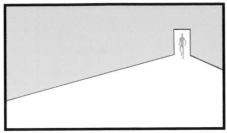

Here are two shots: one is a wide shot of an actor standing in a doorway, and the second is a close-up of the same actor. In the wide shot, the point-of-attention is the actor in the doorway, and in the close-up, the point-of-attention is the actor's eyes.

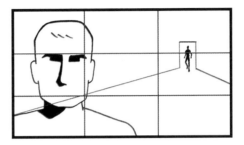

If the two shots are superimposed, the different attention points are visible. Editing these two shots together will create contrast of continuum of movement because on the cut, the audience's point-of-attention jumps from Q3 (screen right) to Q4 (screen left). This generates contrast of continuum of movement.

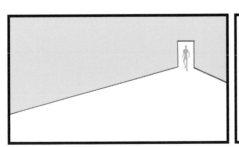

One of the shots can be recomposed to create affinity of continuum of movement from shot to shot.

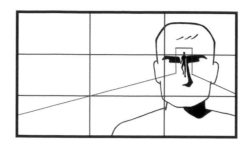

Superimposing the shots shows how the points of attention match. This creates affinity of continuum of movement because the audience's point-of-attention will not move on the cut or edit. The point-of-attention remains in the same quadrant for both shots.

The continuum of movement within a shot or in a series of shots can be planned in a storyboard. The following storyboard panels illustrate these contrasts and affinities.

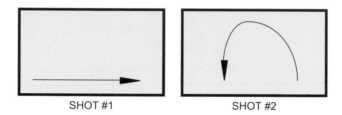

SHOT #1   SHOT #2

Shot #1 indicates an object's movement (a moving car, a running actor, etc.) beginning in Q7 (lower left) and moving in a straight line to Q9 (lower right). The curved movement in Shot #2 begins in the same spot where the movement ended in Shot #1.

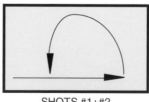

SHOTS #1+#2

When superimposed, the continuum of movement is revealed. The audience's point-of-attention will move with Shot #1 and smoothly transition into Shot #2. The two movements when edited together will merge into one continuous track or line. This is an example of affinity of continuum of movement from shot to shot.

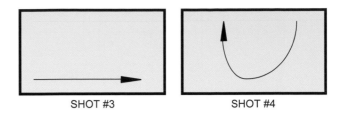

SHOT #3   SHOT #4

Shots #3 and #4 illustrate contrast of continuum of movement from shot to shot. In Shot #3 the object moves from Q7 (lower left) to Q9 (lower right). On the cut to Shot #4, the audience's point-of-attention must quickly move to Q3 (upper right) to find the next moving object. The audience's unaided shift of attention on the cut creates contrast of continuum of movement.

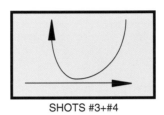

SHOTS #3+#4

When Shots #3 and #4 are superimposed, the contrast of continuum of movement is apparent. There are two completely separate lines or tracks generated by the moving objects.

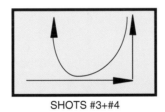

SHOTS #3+#4

But the combination of Shots #3 and #4 actually has three lines. Two are created by the moving objects in frame, and a third line is generated by the audience's point-of-attention moving from the first object in Q9 (lower right) to the second object in Q3 (upper right).

Control of Movement in Production

The importance of continuum of movement in a shot or series of shots can be planned in a storyboard. The arrows in each storyboard picture indicate the movement of an object in the frame.

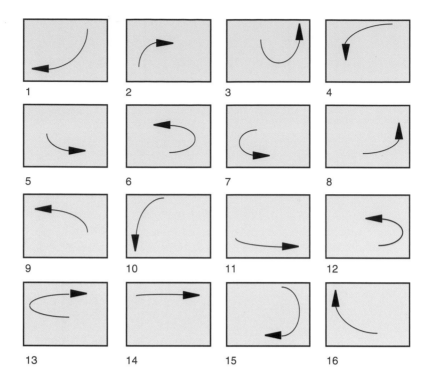

In Storyboard #1, notice the curved (curvilinear) tracks and the affinity of continuum of movement. The viewer's point-of-attention will be left off in one shot and then picked up in the next shot in the same quadrant.

STORYBOARD #1   SHOTS 1-16

Combining all the pictures into a single frame reveals the linear motif created by the tracks of object movement from shot to shot. The eye's path of movement is choreographed around the frame in a circular manner. The affinity of continuum of movement reduces visual intensity and smoothes the transitions from shot to shot.

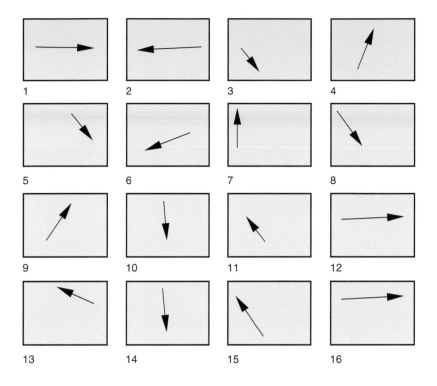

1
2
3
4
5
6
7
8
9
10
11
12
13
14
15
16

Storyboard #2 uses straight lines or tracks instead of curves, but there's still affinity of continuum of movement. The incoming movement starts in the same quadrant where the outgoing movement stops.

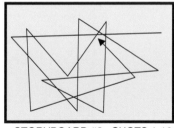

STORYBOARD #2 SHOTS 1-16

When all the pictures are superimposed into a single frame, the linear motif is revealed. The straight, angular lines or tracks create a smooth continuity, generated by the affinity of continuum of movement.

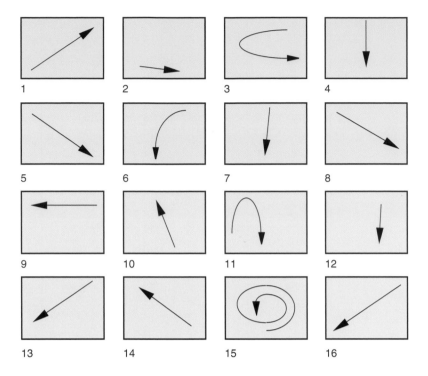

Storyboard #3 is full of contrasts. There's contrast of straight and curved lines; diagonal, horizontal, and vertical tracks; and contrast of continuum of movement. The point-of-attention quadrant is never the same from shot to shot. On each editorial cut, the audience must shift their point-of-attention to another quadrant to find the next moving object.

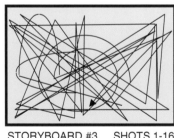

STORYBOARD #3   SHOTS 1-16

This is the linear motif of the pictures in Storyboard #3, which is most intense because it uses so much visual contrast. The total number of lines has doubled. Not only are there lines generated by the tracks of the moving objects, but there are also lines produced by the track of the audience's moving point-of-attention.

Storyboards #1, #2, and #3 create a visual progression. Based purely on the amount of contrast and affinity, Storyboard #1 is least intense because it uses visual affinity. Storyboard #3 is the most intense, because of the visual contrasts of line quality, direction, and continuum of movement.

Continuum of movement is planned and created by the director and cinematographer, but ultimately comes under the control of the editor. Obviously, the editor's continuum control will be limited by the shots produced during production, but the editor who understands continuum of movement has an additional tool to manipulate the intensity of scenes and sequences.

Once in the editing room, it's easy to determine where the audience is looking in any shot. View the shot and be aware of your own point-of-attention. Stop the footage and mark the viewing screen with a grease pencil. You've probably found the correct point-of-attention based on your own natural instincts. If you're still not sure, watch the footage without sound, in a darkened room, and your visual intuition will usually take over and direct your eye to the same point on the screen that will attract the audience.

Continuum of movement is a nearly invisible visual component that has an enormous impact on the audience. As the screen size increases, so does the chance for greater contrast of continuum of movement. As the screen shrinks in size, the chances for contrast of continuum diminish.

Contrast and affinity of continuum of movement affect the intensity or dynamics of edited sequences. Visual intensity will increase as more contrast of continuum is used and visual intensity will decrease if there is affinity of continuum of movement.

Affinity of continuum guides the audience's point-of-attention as they look around the frame. The picture maker can manipulate the audience and control the area of the screen they watch (a critical factor in television commercials).

In a completed film, the audience should be unaware of the editing. Affinity of continuum of movement improves visual continuity, and is such a powerful visual tool that it can disguise visual errors including continuity mistakes and screen direction problems. Affinity makes visual events and transitions appear continuous and smooth.

Any contrast creates intensity. Contrast of continuum of movement can be visually disjointed, jarring, and abrupt. The audience can become agitated or excited when forced to quickly move their attention to different quadrants of the screen without apparent motivation. Contrast of continuum of movement separates actions and removes transitions. As the contrast of continuum increases, so will the visual intensity of the sequence.

Films to Watch

Continuum of Movement

> **Ninotchka** (1939)
>
> Directed by Ernst Lubitsch
>
> Written by Charles Brackett, Billy Wilder, and Walter Reisch
>
> Photographed by William Daniels
>
> Art Direction by Cedric Gibbons

> **Lawrence of Arabia** (1962)
>
> Directed by David Lean
>
> Written by Robert Bolt
>
> Photographed by Frederick Francis
>
> Production Design by John Box

> **Goodfellas** (1990)
>
> Directed by Martin Scorsese
>
> Written by Martin Scorsese and Nicholas Pileggi
>
> Photographed by Michael Ballhaus
>
> Production Design by Kristi Zea

> **Touch of Evil** (1958)
>
> Directed by Orson Welles
>
> Written by Orson Welles
>
> Photographed by Russel Metty
>
> Art Direction by Robert Clatworthy

Camera Movement

> **Das Boot** (1981)
>
> Directed by Wolfgang Peterson
>
> Written by Wolfgang Peterson
>
> Photographed by Jost Vacano
>
> Production Design by Klaus Doldinger

The Verdict (1982)

Directed by Sidney Lumet

Written by David Mamet

Photographed by Andrzej Bartkowiak

Production Design by Edward Pisoni

Collateral (2004)

Directed by Michael Mann

Written by Stuart Beattie

Photographed by Dion Beebe and Paul Cameron

Production Design by David Wasco

Object Movement

Gold Diggers of 1935 (1935)

Directed by Busby Berkeley

Written by Manuel Seff and Peter Milne

Photographed by George Burns

Art Direction by Anton Grot

The Fast and the Furious (2001)

Directed by Rob Cohen

Written by Gary Scott Thompson, Eric Bergquist, and David Ayer

Photographed by Ericson Core

Production Design by Waldemar Kalinowski

The Matrix (1999–2003)

Directed by Andy and Larry Wachowski

Written by Andy and Larry Wachowski

Photographed by Bill Pope

Production Design by Owen Paterson

Casino Royale (2006)

Directed by Martin Campbell

Written by Neal Purvis, Robert Wade, and Paul Haggis

Photographed by Phil Meheux

Production Design by Peter Lamont

8

Rhythm

Rhythm is easy to experience but difficult to describe. Rhythm is perceived in three different ways: we hear it, we see it, and we feel it. We're most familiar with rhythm we can hear, so we will define rhythm's subcomponents using the sound from a musician's metronome. A metronome's ticking sound creates beats that we recognize as rhythm. Every rhythm is made up of three subcomponents: alternation, repetition, and tempo.

Alternation

A metronome's rhythm exists because there's a sound followed by a moment of silence. Without alternation between sound and silence there can't be any rhythm.

There are many types of alternation. There is alternation between sound and silence, high- and low-pitched sounds, or loud and quiet sounds, for example.

The sounds of a ticking clock, walking feet, and a bouncing ball reveal their rhythms because of the alternation. White noise, like the sounds of a constantly humming fan or a waterfall, doesn't have rhythm because it lacks alternation.

Repetition

The alternation of the metronome must repeat. A single beat from a metronome doesn't produce a rhythm. Sound – silence – sound – silence – sound creates a rhythm.

We can't recognize the rhythm of walking feet if the walker takes only one step. If a ball bounces only once, it won't create a rhythm.

Tempo

A metronome has a speed control to change the time between sounds. Any rhythm has a rate of alternation and repetition that is called tempo. The rhythmic difference between walking and running is tempo. A long interval of time creates a slow tempo and a short interval of time creates a fast tempo.

A metronome produces a rhythm we hear, but now we must define rhythm we can see. Visual rhythm is defined by the same subcomponents of alternation, repetition, and tempo. Visual rhythm can be created by stationary objects, moving objects, and editorial cutting.

Rhythm of Stationary Objects

Visual rhythm is created by placing stationary objects in the frame. This is called composition. Simply stated, composition is the arrangement of objects within the frame.

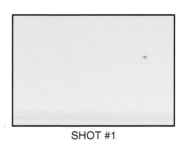

SHOT #1

Shot #1 is an empty frame. It is the visual equivalent of white noise. This shot has no visual rhythm because there isn't any alternation, repetition, or tempo.

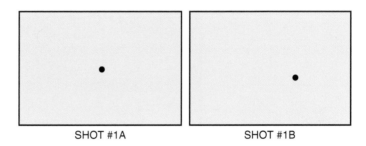

SHOT #1A   SHOT #1B

An object—a dot—has been added, and now the empty frame has a visual rhythm. Shots #1A and #1B both have rhythm, but Shot #1B appears more intense than Shot #1A.

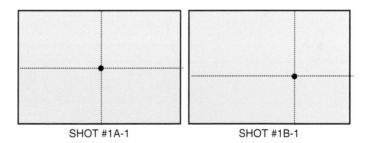

SHOT #1A-1   SHOT #1B-1

The reason for Shot #1B's greater intensity is revealed when lines are drawn through the dot. Shot #1A-1 divides the frame into four equal areas, and #1B-1 divides the frame into four unequal areas. The Principle of Contrast of Affinity tells us that affinity (Shot #1A-1 is four equal areas) reduces visual intensity, and contrast (Shot #1B-1 is four unequal areas) increases visual intensity. The arrangement of objects in the frame (composition) and the lines created by these objects is the key to understanding visual rhythm in stationary objects.

SHOT #2

When a single object, a gray rectangle, is placed in the frame it generates alternation and repetition, creating a rhythm.

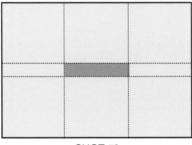

SHOT #3

Extending the sides of the gray rectangle with dotted lines reveals how the rhythm is produced. The dotted lines have divided the frame into smaller areas. The vertical and horizontal lines can be analyzed separately for their visual rhythm and then combined.

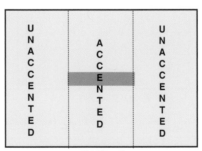

SHOT #4

The vertical lines, created by the gray rectangle, have divided the frame into thirds. There is alternation between these thirds. The center third is a dominant, or accented, beat because it contains the gray rectangle. The thirds on the left and right are unaccented, because they don't contain any objects. Just as sound rhythm alternates between sound and silence, Shot #4 illustrates how the visual rhythm alternates between accented and unaccented areas of the frame. Sometimes the term "positive space" is used for accented areas, and "negative space" is used for unaccented areas. The two unaccented areas create the needed repetition.

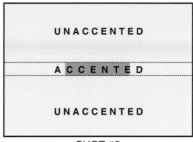
SHOT #5

There is also alternation in the horizontal divisions created by the gray rectangle. The narrow accented band in the center alternates with the larger unaccented areas above and below it. The two unaccented areas create repetition.

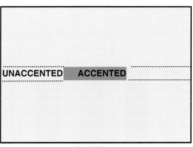
SHOT #6

Even the narrow center band can be divided into alternating thirds. The gray rectangle and the narrow bands to its left and right create alternation. The gray rectangle is accented, and the two side areas are unaccented.

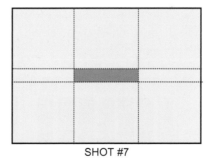
SHOT #7

Combining the vertical and horizontal lines reveals the complete visual rhythm. The dotted lines show how the frame has been divided into a variety of areas.

Dividing the frame has also created tempo. The viewer scans the entire frame and makes several instantaneous measurements. The distance between the gray rectangle and the frame lines and the proportion of the divided areas of the frame are measured by the eye, resulting in a sense of visual rhythm. The tempo in Drawing #7 is slow.

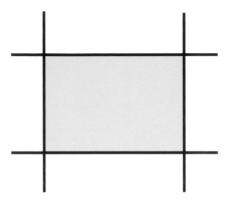

The frame itself has four important lines that can contribute to the visual rhythm. The frame's vertical and horizontal lines help define the visual repetition created by lines within the frame.

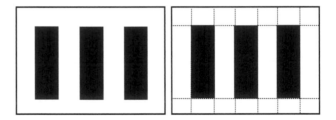

Now the frame is divided into more parts, and the tempo increases. The three stationary (nonmoving) squares represent a moderate rhythm. A viewer is aware of the frame lines and when dotted lines are added between the rectangles, the alternation, repetition, and tempo are revealed. There is alternation between the rectangles, the space around them, and the frame lines. There is repetition in the rectangles themselves, and there is a faster tempo created by the number of frame divisions.

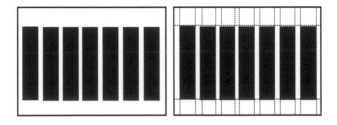

The alternation, repetition, and the tempo are faster because there are more rectangles that divide the frame into more parts. But we don't make films or videos about rectangles, so these rhythm concepts must be related back to the real world.

An actor has replaced the rectangles, but the subcomponents of visual rhythm are still the same. A rectangle substitutes for the actor and reveals lines that divide the frame into separate areas. There is alternation. The actor becomes the accent surrounded by unaccented areas. There is repetition, because the frame is divided into more than one area, and the tempo is slow. This picture has a slow, slightly irregular visual rhythm. If the actor was centered in the frame, the rhythm would be slow and regular.

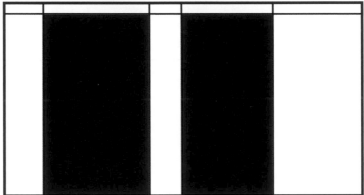

This two-shot divides the frame into more areas. Adding rectangles and lines reveals the shot's alternation, repetition, and tempo. The shot has a moderate, regular rhythm.

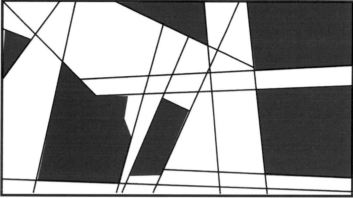

This shot has a fast, irregular rhythm. The graphic of rectangles and lines reveals how the visual rhythm really looks. The divided areas of the frame are unequal, so the tempo changes as the viewer looks around the frame.

Rhythm of Moving Objects

An object must move in relation to the frame line to create movement. Most object movement does not create rhythm.

There are two types of rhythm in moving objects: primary and secondary. The movement of a whole object creates a primary rhythm. When a part of the whole object moves independently, a secondary rhythm can be created.

Primary Rhythm

There are four ways a moving object can create a primary visual rhythm:

- Entering and exiting the frame
- Moving in front of or behind another object
- Moving and stopping
- Changing direction

The movement of a ball can demonstrate the following four methods of creating primary visual rhythm.

Entering and Exiting the Frame

When an object crosses the frame line, a single visual beat is created.

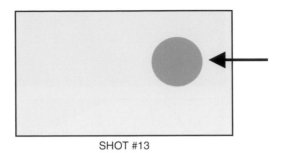

SHOT #13

The ball entering frame cannot create visual rhythm because a single beat lacks alternation, repetition, and tempo.

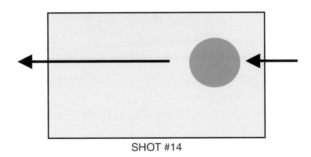

SHOT #14

A rhythm may be created if the ball enters and exits the frame because it produces alternation and repetition. The frame lines act as visual accents in contrast to the unaccented frame area. Repetition occurs because there are two frame lines, and the ball crosses both of them.

If several objects enter and exit the frame, a more complicated visual rhythm is created. Each object's entrance and exit produces an additional visual beat.

Passing Another Object

A visual beat is created when a moving object passes in front of or behind other objects.

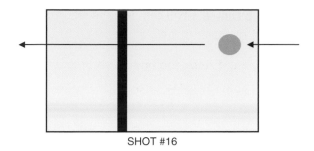

SHOT #16

The ball enters frame, moves past a FG or BG object (drawn here as a pole), and exits frame. As the ball passes the pole it will produce a visual beat like the ones created when the ball entered and exited the frame.

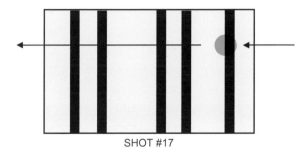

SHOT #17

Adding more FG or BG objects increases the alternation, repetition, and tempo. The moving object emphasizes the visual rhythm created by the stationary objects. As the moving object passes a stationary FG or BG object, that existing visual beat is made stronger.

Moving and Stopping

If an object starts and stops moving in frame more than once, a visual rhythm is produced.

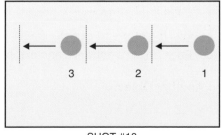

SHOT #18

The stopping and starting ball has alternation, repetition, and tempo just like a metronome.

Changing Direction

A change in direction, if it happens more than once, will also create a visual rhythm.

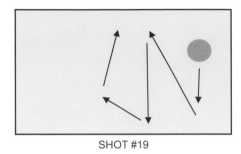

SHOT #19

Each change in the direction of the ball's movement will produce visual alternation, repetition, and tempo.

Secondary Rhythm

A secondary rhythm is generated by the movement of part of an object that already generates a primary rhythm.

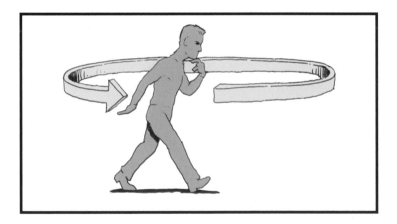

The Primary Rhythm is a person pacing back and forth; the Secondary Rhythm is the person's moving legs and feet.

There is a primary rhythm as the person stops and starts or changes direction, but there is also a secondary rhythm produced by the person's moving legs and feet that has alternation, repetition, and tempo completely separate from the primary rhythm.

There is rhythm in editing. Every time the editor makes a cut, a new rhythmic beat can be produced.

Editorial rhythm has the same basic components of alternation, repetition, and tempo. Editorial alternation occurs because the cut is the accent or beat and the time between cuts is the unaccented alternate. The greater the visual contrast in the visual components from shot to shot, the stronger the beat produced by the cut.

These two pictures have contrast of tone. One is extremely dark and the other is bright. When these two shots are intercut, the tonal contrast from shot to shot will create a strong rhythmic beat.

These two shots are similar in space, line, tone, and color. Their visual affinity will make the rhythmic beats created by intercutting less intense.

Two kinds of visual repetition occur when a cut is made. The first type is editorial repetition. It occurs because a beat is produced by every cut or edit. With each cut, the pattern of repetition is continued.

The second type is pictorial repetition, which occurs when the same shots are repeated. If the editor is intercutting two close-ups in a conversation scene, a repetition occurs. The audience sees two alternating shots repeated again and again. The more often the same shots are repeated, the more apparent the repetition becomes, creating visual affinity. Visual intensity diminishes each time the same shot is repeated.

Finally there is editorial tempo. Any series of edits will have a tempo that remains constant, speeds up, or slows down. It's easier for an audience to sense visual rhythm in sequences with faster cutting tempos. As the time between edits increases, the audience's sense of the editorial tempo diminishes. What is actually a slow tempo may read as no tempo at all, because the time length between edits is too long. It is difficult for an audience to sense editorial repetition if the edits are more than approximately ten seconds apart.

The Principle of Contrast & Affinity can be controlled through editing. Editing is the picture maker's last chance to manipulate the structure of the story, the nature of the actors' performances, and the basic visual components. The ultimate control of the Principle of Contrast & Affinity is in the hands of the editor, but an editor can use it only within the confines of the footage that has been produced.

The Event

A single action, a scene or a group of scenes, or an entire story can be called an event. This event can be simple (a hand opens a door) or complex (a person is born, lives to be 90 years old, and dies). Any event can be broken down into a number of subevents.

The event is simple: "a hand opens a door." The subevents that make up the event are:

1. The hand reaches for the doorknob.

2. The hand grasps the knob.

3. The hand turns the knob.

4. The door latch moves.

5. The door begins to open.

6. The hand releases the knob.

7. The door completely opens.

Listing the subevents allows us to understand each part of the overall event. On a time line, the event looks like this:

Each number on the time line represents a subevent from "a hand opens a door."

Breaking down an event into subevents reveals the parts of the event. It helps the picture maker find the event's story structure and discover the best way to photograph it. Any event can be photographed continuously or fragmentedly.

The Continuous Event

When an event is photographed in a continuous manner, there are no camera cuts. As the event progresses in time moving from one subevent to the next, the camera will run continuously. The camera can remain stationary or it can move, but the event and all its subevents will be photographed in one continuous take. When the event ends, the camera is shut off. First-person video games are good examples of continuous events. The screen is the player's view and the playing event happens continuously. When the event is over, the player has failed or completed the game.

In the continuous event, editing will be unnecessary because the entire event is captured in only one shot. The editor will not have control over the rhythm or anything else in the shot. The visual rhythm of the scene must be controlled as the event is being photographed.

The Fragmented Event

Alternatively, an event can be photographed in a fragmented manner where it is broken down into separate shots. Each subevent is given its own shot or several shots. This is usually called shooting *coverage*, and typically includes camera angles like a master shot, full shot, medium shots, close-ups, inserts, and cutaways, which, when edited together, reconstruct the subevents into a single event.

Greater visual component contrast in the fragmented subevents will increase the intensity of the visual structure. Using affinity in the fragmented subevents will lower the visual intensity. A skilled editor understands visual structure and can pick the fragmented subevents most appropriate for the story structure.

Continuous and fragmented events are opposites, and there are good reasons to use both techniques.

Visual Emphasis

Each type of event control will emphasize the other. Fragmentation will have more emphasis when it has been preceded by a continuous sequence. Conversely, a continuously filmed sequence will gain emphasis if it has been preceded by a fragmented sequence.

Contrast and Affinity Control

When filming is continuous, the ability to specifically orchestrate contrast and affinity is limited, because the camera can't be turned off during the event. A fragmented sequence makes control of contrast and affinity easier. Since fragmenting allows an event to be broken down into a series of subevents or separate shots, the visual components can be rearranged for each new shot. This means that the picture makers can create changes of contrast or affinity for any visual component in every shot. In postproduction, the editor can further arrange the fragmented shots to enhance the visual contrast or affinity.

Editorial Event Control

A fragmented event allows the editor to rearrange the order of the subevents. A continuously filmed scene will not permit editorial restructuring.

Editorial Rhythmic Control

Fragmenting permits the rhythm of a scene to be altered. The tempo of subevents can be increased or decreased through editing.

Visual Variety

Continuous and fragmented shooting is an important factor in the overall visual variety of a production. If an audience is going to watch a two-hour film, how long can they watch something that's only fragmented? At what point will fragmenting lose its visual impact? Sometimes a visual structure needs continuous/fragmented variation just to keep the visuals from becoming dull.

Finding a Rhythm

Fragmenting an event is often difficult for actors who are trying to find the overall rhythm of a scene or sequence. The continuous event allows the actors to develop rhythms that might not emerge during short subevents.

Directorial Choice

The story can suggest a continuous or fragmented approach. A scene that involves real time might play better as a continuous shot. A scene involving complex action might best be filmed in a fragmented manner so that the editor can manipulate the physical complexities. Sometimes an event is so complicated that it can be understood only when the subevents are fragmented. Other times, an event feels more real if it is filmed continuously, without editorial manipulation.

A continuous or fragmented technique has no strict rules for its use. You must evaluate the nature of every scene and decide what technique will best serve the story.

Rhythmic Patterns

Different stories have different rhythms. It's possible to draw a flow-line to represent the rhythms of a story that can help you discover the visual rhythms for a production.

This flow-line represents the rhythms of stories that alternate between great rhythmic peaks and valleys. The *Godfather*, *Ran*, *Raging Bull*, *Lawrence of Arabia*, and *Citizen Kane* are examples of this type of overall visual rhythm.

This staccato rhythm represents a faster, more energetic rhythm often used in physical comedies. A *Night at the Opera*, *Bringing Up Baby*, *Airplane*, and *Back to the Future* have visual rhythms suggested by this flow-line.

This slowly undulating flow-line has a slower rhythm that makes gradual, milder changes. *Howards End*, *Hannah and Her Sisters*, *Wings of the Dove*, and *The Sixth Sense* follow this rhythmic pattern.

Every story has a rhythmic flow-line pattern. It may be a combination of these examples or a different line altogether. Drawing a flow line for the rhythm is an easy way to visualize the rhythmic feeling of your production. This idea will be elaborated on in Chapter 9.

In the days of silent films, orchestras often played music during filming to help actors create the proper mood and rhythm of a scene. Today, because we record sound, the use of music on the set during filming is difficult; however, it's possible to rehearse with music or even a metronome.

Here are some standard metronome settings:

Metronome Setting	Number of Beats
240	4 every second
120	2 every second
60	1 every second
30	1 every two seconds

Using a metronome can help control the rhythm of dialogue, movement, or mood during production.

Contrast and Affinity

There are several ways that rhythm can create contrast or affinity. Remember that contrast and affinity can occur within the shot, from shot to shot, and from sequence to sequence.

Slow/Fast

A rhythm's tempo can range in speed from slow to fast. The tempo can be produced by stationary objects, moving objects, or the editor's cutting pattern.

Almost any meaning can be associated with any tempo. A faster tempo may communicate happiness, excitement, or comedic intent. A slower rhythm may suggest calm, sadness, or tragedy. Assigning general emotional values to any visual component is dangerous because it can lead to stereotypes. If controlled properly, any meaning can be associated with any rhythmic tempo.

The editor will create rhythm by cutting the fragmented scene together and by manipulating the rhythm of the scene itself. The editor can speed up or slow down the rhythm through editing.

Regular/Irregular

Rhythm is also classified in terms of being regular and irregular. When the tempo remains constant, the rhythm is regular. If the tempo changes often enough, the rhythm can develop an irregular pattern.

Because regularity has a predictable pattern, it usually communicates affinity or lack of intensity. An irregular rhythm generally increases the rhythmic contrast and produces greater visual intensity or dynamic.

The rhythmic beats in the first example, created by the vertical windows, create a slower, regular rhythm. The picture has rhythmic affinity. The second example, the bookstore, has a faster irregular rhythm and more visual contrast. The viewer's eye jumps quickly around the frame from the actor's face, to the ceiling lights, the light patterns on the wall, the books and the background actors.

Controlling Rhythm During Production

Rhythmic control is complex. Here are some guidelines for controlling it during production.

1. **Watch the lines**. Linear motif is the arrangement of stationary lines in the picture. It is also the key to finding the visual rhythm. Once you find the lines (using all the methods described in Chapter 4), evaluate them to find the rhythm. If there are only a few evenly spaced lines, the rhythm is probably slow and regular. As the number of lines increases, the visual rhythm gets faster. If the lines are uneven, it's probably an irregular rhythm.

2. **Don't confuse rhythm with movement**. Most visual rhythms are created by stationary objects. A fast movement may not have a fast rhythm (or any rhythm at all). A movement can be slow or fast, but that is a separate visual component.

3. **Find rhythm in movement**. Certain types of movements do create visual rhythm. The rhythmic beat will increase in intensity as the moving object gets larger in frame.

4. **Find the rhythm for a scene**. If you have dialogue, find the sound's rhythm first and then let it define the visual rhythm. If there is no dialogue, using other sounds or music can help you discover the visual rhythm.

5. **Plan the editing**. Decide how much editing will be involved in a scene or sequence. This will affect the amount of fragmentation or coverage you'll need.

Films to Watch

Rhythmic Control

Each of these films has a distinct rhythmic control of the sound and visual components. Watch the films with the sound on, and then again with the sound off, and the rhythmic structure of the pictures and the editing will become clear.

Raging Bull (1980)

Directed by Martin Scorsese

Written by Paul Schrader and Mardik Martin

Photographed by Michael Chapman

Art Direction by Gene Rudolph

Edited by Thelma Schoonmaker

Rumble Fish (1983)

Directed by Francis Ford Coppola

Screenplay by Francis Ford Coppola

Photographed by Steve Burum

Production Design by Dean Tavoularis

Edited by Barry Malkin

Barry Lyndon (1975)

Directed by Stanley Kubrick

Written by Stanley Kubrick

Photographed by John Alcott

Production Design by Ken Adam

Rashomon (1951)

Directed by Akira Kurosawa

Written by Akira Kurosawa

Photographed by Kazuo Miyagawa

Art Direction by H. Motsumoto

The Last Picture Show (1971)

Directed by Peter Bogdanovich

Written by Peter Bogdanovich and Larry McMurtry

Photographed by Robert Surtees

Production Design by Polly Platt

Edited by Don Cambern

The Continuous and Fragment Event

Touch of Evil (1958)

Directed by Orson Welles

Written by Orson Welles

Photographed by Russell Metty

Art Direction by Robert Clatworthy

Edited by Edward Curtiss

Goodfellas (1990)

Directed by Martin Scorsese

Written by Nicholas Pileggi

Photographed by Michael Ballhaus

Production Design by Christie Zea

Edited by Thelma Schoonmaker

The Untouchables (1987)

Directed by Brian DePalma

Written by David Mamet

Photographed by Steven Burum

Production Design by Patrizia Von Brandenstein

Edited by Jerry Greenberg

Man on Fire (2004)

Directed by Tony Scott

Screenplay by Brian Helgeland

Photographed by Paul Cameron

Production Design by Benjamin Fernandez and Chris Seagers

Edited by Christian Wagner

Run, Lola, Run (1999)

Directed by Tom Tykwer

Written by Tom Tykwer

Photographed by Frank Griebe

Production Design by Alexander Manasse

Edited by Mathilde Bonnefoy

JFK (1991)

Directed by Oliver Stone

Written by Oliver Stone and Zachary Sklar

Photographed by Robert Richardson

Production Design by Victor Kempster

Edited by Joe Hutshing and Pietro Scalia

The Russian Ark (2002)

Directed by Alexander Sokurov

Written by Anatoli Nikiforov

Photographed by Tilman Büttner

Art Direction by Natalya Kochergina

Traffic (2000)

Directed by Steven Soderbergh

Screenplay by Stephen Gaghan

Photographed by Steven Soderbergh

Production Design by Philip Messina

These films use continuous and fragmented techniques to create a variety of visual rhythms.

Story and Visual Structure

The Key Relationship

Before visual structure can be used correctly, some basic story structure concepts must be understood. This chapter will not attempt to explain story structure; instead, it defines some terms that will help link visual and story structure together.

A story has three basic parts:

- Exposition (beginning)
- Conflict (middle)
- Resolution (end)

Exposition

The beginning of a story is called the *exposition*. Exposition can be defined as the facts needed to begin the story. These facts include (but are not limited to) the identity of the main characters, their plot situation, location, and time period. If the audience is not given the facts they need (or think they need), they can never become involved in the story because they're distracted with trying to fill in the missing exposition.

The fundamentals of exposition were first described and used by Aristotle in ancient Greek theatre, but the examples in this book will be confined to feature films. Over the years, scriptwriters have developed various techniques for using exposition in their stories.

A long-standing expositional technique is the title card or crawl. John Ford's *The Searchers* (1956) begins with a title card that simply states the exposition for the time and place: "Texas 1868."

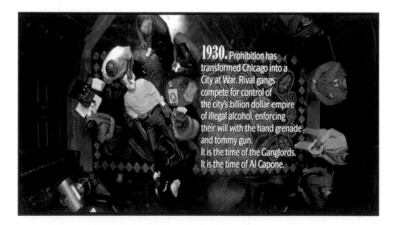

The Untouchables (1987) opens with a title card explaining the 1930 political situation in Chicago.

A crawl is a longer expositional statement about the upcoming story. Films like *Air Force*, *Boy's Town*, many documentaries, and all the *Star Wars* movies begin with expository crawls.

Voice-over narration is a common tool for exposition. Orson Welles narrated some of his films (a convention he brought from radio) to give the audience the facts they needed to begin the story. In the exposition of *The Magnificent Ambersons* (1942), Welles tells the audience about the main characters and the social customs of the era. *Network* (1976) uses a narrator to present exposition about the news division of a television network. Billy Wilder's *The Apartment* (1960) begins with narration by the main character, C.C. Baxter, who introduces the unethical situation in his apartment.

The exposition in *Casablanca* (1942) begins with a map of Europe. In 1942, audiences were unfamiliar with Casablanca so narration explains the city's location and political importance. The exposition continues with an announcement about stolen passports followed by a montage of the corrupt characters living among the tourists in Casablanca.

Sometimes the narration continues throughout the story, as in *The Shawshank Redemption* (1994). In *Little Big Man* (1970), Dustin Hoffman appears in the exposition as the elderly Jack Crabb. His story, told in flashback, shows Jack as a young man, but the narration continues in the old man's voice. The mad composer Salieri narrates *Amadeus* (1984) in the same way. Fred McMurray's character, Walter Neff, narrates the entire film in *Double Indemnity* (1944). In *Ferris Bueller's Day Off* (1986), Ferris narrates by talking directly to the camera, filling in exposition as well as commenting on the story situation.

Exposition is sometimes handled in a more complex manner. *Citizen Kane's* (1941) exposition is the elaborate "News on the March" newsreel. It presents a narrated chronological history of Charles Foster Kane's life. The story then revisits Kane's life in a series of nonlinear flashbacks that could be confusing, but the facts needed to understand it are presented in the exposition. Sidney Lumet's *Murder on the Orient Express* (1974) has two expositions. The first is a flashback, an expositional prologue that explains tragic events that occurred five years before the story begins. The second exposition introduces the entire cast of characters as they board the Orient Express train. In the exposition of Sergio Leone's *The Good, the Bad, and the Ugly* (1966), each of the three cowboys is introduced with an expository scene and then a title card reading: "The Good," or "The Bad," or "The Ugly." The exposition reveals the personalities of the three cowboys, the story conflict, the location, and the time period.

As a story develops, additional exposition is sometimes needed to introduce new characters, elaborate on new situations, or give the audience information that was withheld at the opening exposition. In Hitchcock's *North by Northwest* (1959), the Intelligence Agency is used to reveal additional exposition during the story's conflict. The complex Harry Potter stories constantly reveal new information with expositional scenes throughout the story.

Conflict and Climax

The middle part of a story is called the *conflict*. When the story begins, there's usually little or no conflict, and as the story develops, the conflict increases in intensity.

A conflict can be internal or external. An internal conflict involves an emotional struggle. In *The Apartment* (1960), there are two internal struggles: C.C. Baxter's moral dilemma about the use of his apartment and his unsuccessful romance with Miss Kubelik. In *Howards End* (1992), the internal conflict deals with the emotional problems created by England's socioeconomic class system in 1910.

Remains of the Day (1993) is about a British manor house butler who refuses to recognize that his job is a dying custom. His internal conflict makes him hide from the changing world despite the warning of his friends.

Honesty versus corruption is the internal conflict in *Serpico* (1973). The honest policeman Frank Serpico tries unsuccessfully to fight growing political corruption. His conflict is trying to remain honest in a corrupt environment.

An external conflict involves a physical situation. The external or physical conflict in *Jaws* concerns a town and a shark. Hunters want to kill the shark before it ruins the lucrative summer tourist trade. The *Kill Bill* (2003, 2004) films are a series of external conflicts based on revenge. The *Back to the Future* films (1985, 1990) involve external, physical conflicts caused by time travel.

A story conflict can be both internal and external. In *Casablanca*, trying to find airplane transportation out of the country is the external conflict. The internal emotional conflict involves Rick's love for Ilsa. As the conflicts intensify, the two intertwine. In *Citizen Kane* the external conflict is the reporter's physical search to discover the meaning of "Rosebud." In his search, the reporter stumbles onto internal, emotional conflicts between Kane and his wives, friends, and enemies. Richard Brooks' *In Cold Blood* (1967) is an external conflict searching for a pair of murderers and an internal conflict about understanding their motivations. *Star Wars* (1977) involves the external conflict of defeating Darth Vader and Luke's internal conflict to find the force and conquer his self-esteem problem. Martin Scorsese's *The Departed* (2006) has an external conflict of finding the informant and an internal conflict about personal morality.

A conflict builds in intensity as the story progresses. The most intense part of a conflict is the climax. At the climax, the main character must choose a path and win or lose. At the climax, the internal or external conflict must end. The climax of *Jaws* is the final action sequence at sea and the shark's death. In *The*

Apartment, Baxter quits his job and finds love. At the climax of *Howards End*, Henry Bast is killed. The climax of *In Cold Blood* is the flashback to the Clutter family murders.

Depending on your specific ideas about story structure, you may adjust the exact placement of the climax. No matter how you define it, the climax still occurs at the height of the conflict.

Resolution

The resolution provides a place for the story to finish. The audience needs time to recover from the intensity of the climax and reflect on the story's conflict. Also, secondary plot situations and characters may need time to fully complete their story.

The resolution in *Casablanca* takes place at the airport after Rick has seen Ilsa and Victor fly safely away. The conflict is over. Rick finds the police chief and it's business as usual as they walk off into the darkness.

The physical conflict in *Citizen Kane* appears to end without an answer to the mystery word "Rosebud." The resolution shows the reporters leaving but the audience gets to see Kane's childhood sled inscribed with "Rosebud" as it disappears into an incinerator. This final shot of the resolution explains Kane and his lost childhood.

The resolution in *Jaws* is quick and simple. The shark has been killed and the police chief is reunited with the scientist. The ocean is once again safe for swimmers. In the resolution, the two men calmly swim to shore and the ominous music that signaled the shark's approach is gone.

Hitchcock's *North by Northwest* (1959) has a 20-second resolution. Thornhill lifts Kendall up into the train berth, kisses her, and the train disappears into a tunnel.

When the resolution requires more information, a title card or crawl can be used as in *American Graffiti* (1973) and *Animal House* (1978). These title cards explain what happened to each character after graduating from school. *The Shawshank Redemption*, *Double Indemnity*, and *Father of the Bride* use narration during the resolution to explain the character's feelings and to complete the story.

The Story Structure Graph

Every story, no matter how brief or long, has an exposition, conflict, climax and resolution. The story can be a commercial, a video game, a documentary, a television program, or a feature length film script.

A story usually exists as words written on a page. This is fine if you're reading the story, but a different format is needed to visualize a story's structure. The structure of any story can be charted on a graph.

Graph A

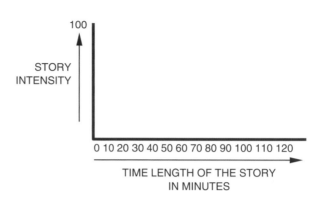

This is a story structure graph. The horizontal axis of Graph A indicates the time length of the story (120 minutes in this example). The vertical axis represents the intensity of the story. Story intensity refers to the degree of conflict in the story. The 0 on the story intensity scale indicates a lack of intensity and 100 indicates maximum intensity.

Graph B

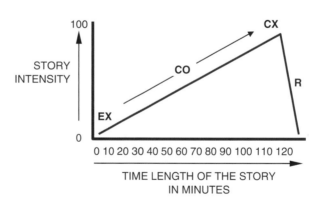

A line drawn on the graph represents the story's intensity. In Graph B, the story begins with the exposition (EX) where the story intensity is low or at 0 on the story intensity scale. The intensity begins to build as the story moves into the conflict (CO). The intensity of the conflict continues to increase until the climax (CX), which is the most intense part of the story conflict. In the resolution (R), the story intensity diminishes and the story ends.

A story begins with exposition, a conflict builds in intensity to a climax and then resolves into an ending. Variations on this story intensity structure graph are discussed later in this chapter.

Chapter 9 • Story and Visual Structure

Graph C

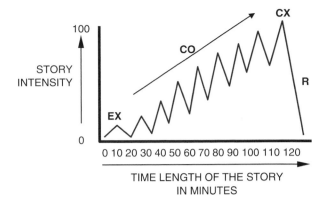

Graph C shows the same overall story intensity as Graph B, but the straight line has been replaced by a jagged line. This jagged line more accurately represents the rises and falls in a story's intensity. Even though the line is jagged, its overall uphill direction is the same as the line in Graph B. The story conflict increases in intensity until it reaches the climax and then quickly decreases in intensity during the resolution. All the films mentioned in this book follow this structure.

North by Northwest (1959)

Hitchcock's *North by Northwest* (1959) is an excellent story structure example because the build of intensifying events is extremely clear. The story can be broken down into sequences on a Story Sequence List.

You must be familiar with *North by Northwest* to understand the following Story Sequence List. If you've not seen this film, you should view it now.

Each sequence in the story has been categorized as exposition, conflict, climax, or resolution:

EX = Exposition

CO = Conflict

CX = Climax

R = Resolution

Story Sequence List

1. EX: Roger Thornhill is a busy executive.

2. CO: Thornhill is kidnapped.

3. EX: Thornhill meets Vandamm at mansion.

4. CO: Drunk driving.

5. CO: Police station and return to mansion.

6. CO: Thornhill finds hotel room and escapes.

7. CO: United Nations.

8. EX: Intelligence Headquarters.

9. CO: Grand Central Station.

10. CO: Thornhill meets Kendall on the train.

11. CO: Chicago train station.

12. CO: Crop duster.

13. CO: Chicago hotel.

14. CO: Auction.

15. EX: The Professor intervenes.

16. CO: Mt. Rushmore Visitor's Center.

17. CO: Kendall and Thornhill reunite.

18. CO: Thornhill in the hospital.

19. CO: Vandamm's house.

20. CO: Walk to Vandamm's plane.

21. CX: Mt. Rushmore.

22. R: Thornhill and Kendall on the train.

Graph D

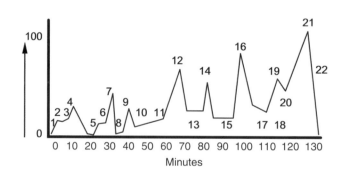

The numbers in Graph D refer to the numbers in the North by Northwest Story Sequence List. The list is used to produce a jagged line that graphs the story's specific changes in intensity. As the story sequences gain intensity, the line reaches higher peaks on the graph.

Sequence #1, the story's exposition, which introduces Roger Thornhill, has no intensity. In Sequence #2, the conflict begins and the story intensity increases when Thornhill is kidnapped. In Sequence #3 and #4 the intensity builds as Thornhill is drugged and forced to drive a car. In Sequence #5 Thornhill recovers at the police station, and the intensity diminishes. The story intensity graph charts every sequence in the story. The most intense peak on the graph is the climax at Mt. Rushmore (#21 on the Story Sequence List). The graph is a visual map of the changes in the story intensity.

You may disagree with this version of how the intensity builds in North by Northwest. Depending upon your ideas about story structure and character, you might locate the intensity rises and falls at different places in the story intensity graph. That's fine. The graphs can plot the intensities in any way that you wish. What is recognized as intensity can differ from story to story, author to author, and director to director. The important concept is to produce a graph that plots the story's intensities.

An intensity graph can be created for an entire story or a sequence within the story. The Crop Duster sequence, like every sequence in *North by Northwest*, has its own intensity build with an exposition, conflict/climax, and resolution. The specifics of the Crop Duster Sequence can be listed and diagramed with a graph.

Crop Duster Sequence List

EX = Exposition

CO = Conflict

CX = Climax

R = Resolution

1. EX: Thornhill arrives by bus.

2. CO: Two cars and a truck pass by.

3. CO: Man arrives and takes a bus.

4. CO: Plane attack #1.

5. CO: Plane attack #2 with machine guns.

6. CO: Thornhill tries to stop a passing car.

7. CO: Plane attack #3 with machine guns.

8. CO: Plane attack #4. No guns.

9. CO: Plane attack #5 with crop dusting chemicals.

10. CX: Plane hits a tanker and explodes.

11. R: Thornhill steals a truck and escapes.

Graph E

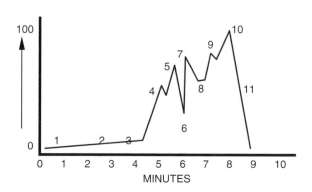

The numbers in Graph E refer to the numbers in the Crop Duster Sequence List. Notice how the structure starts at "0" intensity for about five minutes before the conflict begins to intensify with the attack of the plane. Each time the plane attacks, the intensity increases, building toward the climax when the plane explodes. The resolution is Thornhill driving away in a stolen truck.

Here is a Story Sequence List for *The Bourne Identity* (2002). You must already be familiar with the film to understand this list. If you've not seen this film, you should view it now.

The Bourne Identity **Sequence List**

EX = Exposition

CO = Conflict

CX = Climax

R = Resolution

1. EX: Bourne is rescued at sea.
2. EX: CIA Headquarters with Conklin.
3. EX: Bourne at sea and docks.
4. EX: Switzerland; Park police fight.
5. EX: Wombosi on TV; Abbott and Conklin.
6. EX: Swiss bank safe deposit box.
7. EX: U.S. Embassy lobby.
8. CO: U.S. Embassy chase.
9. CO: Bourne meets Marie.
10. EX: CIA calls in all special agents.
11. CO: Drive to Paris.
12. EX: CIA traces Marie.
13. CO: Roadside diner.
14. CO: Paris apartment arrival.
15. CO: Paris apartment fight.
16. CO: Gare du Nord Station.
17. CO: Police chase the Mini Cooper.
18. EX: Wombosi at the Morgue.
19. CO: Hotel; Marie's haircut.
20. CO: Wombosi is killed.
21. CO: Hotel Regina.
22. EX: Bourne discovers a link between Morgue and Wombosi.
23. CO: Country farm arrival.

24. EX: Country farm; sleeping children.

25. CO: Country farm fight and Marie's exit.

26. CX: Bourne calls Conklin.

27. CX: Meeting on Pont Neuf.

28. CX: Bourne confronts Conklin.

29. CX: Bourne remembers his mission.

30. CX: Staircase fight.

31. R: Conklin is killed.

32. R: Abbott presents a new plan.

33. R: Bourne finds Marie.

Graph F

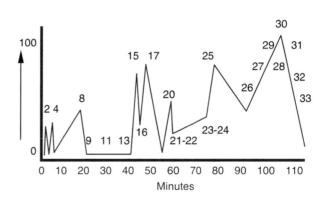

The numbers on Graph F correspond to the numbers of the *The Bourne Identity* Story Sequence List.

The Bourne Identity plot is more complex than *North by Northwest*'s plot, but the same structural elements apply. In the opening sequences all the characters and their basic situations are introduced. Note how Sequence #1 and #4 in the graph are more intense. These brief bursts of intensity are called spikes. Even though Sequence #1 is intense, it's part of the exposition. It gives the audience facts they need to begin the story including the time period, the bullet wounds, and the bank account laser. The exposition continues when Bourne confronts the park police and opens the safe deposit box. The exposition also introduces several characters, locations, and situations that will slowly interconnect as the story progresses. Additional exposition appears later as clues to Bourne's identity and his relationship to Wombosi and the CIA.

The main external/internal conflict is Bourne trying to understand his past and the secondary conflict is the political struggle between Conklin and Abbott at the CIA. The first major conflict is Sequence #8 (Embassy Chase). This sequence is also expositional because it's the first time the audience sees

Bourne reacting under enormous pressure. The conflict continues to intensify as Bourne moves closer to discovering who he is and what he has done.

At the climax, Bourne forces a meeting with Conklin, Bourne remembers his assassination attempt, and he escapes. In the resolution, Conklin is killed and Bourne is reunited with Marie.

Your ideas about the story structure of *The Bourne Identity* may vary from this list. The graph can plot the intensities of any story structure no matter how you interpret the exposition, conflict, climax, and resolution. The important idea is to create a graph that plots the story's intensities. It is the first step to building a visual structure.

Howards End Story Sequence List

This is a breakdown of the story sequences in *Howards End*. You must be familiar with the film to understand the graph. If you've not seen this film you should view it now.

EX = Exposition

CO = Conflict

CX = Climax

R = Resolution

1. EX: Correspondence about Helen Schlegel's failed engagement.
2. EX: Helen and Leonard Bast meet; Wilcox arrives.
3. EX: The Basts live in poverty.
4. CO: Margaret Schlegel and Ruth Wilcox become friends.
5. CO: Ruth dies; her will is destroyed.
6. CO: The Schlegels meet the Basts.
7. CO: Helen takes an interest in Leonard.
8. CO: Henry is attracted to Margaret.
9. CO: Helen tries to help Leonard.
10. CO: Margaret arrives at Howards End.
11. CO: Henry's involvement with Jackie is revealed.
12. CO: Leonard and Helen fall in love.
13. CO: Leonard refuses charity.
14. CO: Helen is pregnant by Leonard.
15. CO: Helen wants to sleep at Howards End.
16. CX: Charles kills Leonard.
17. R: The Schlegels live at Howards End.

Graph G

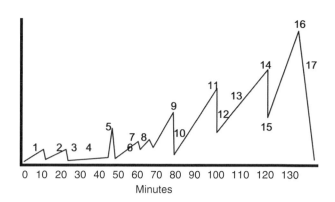

Howards End is a story of three families living in England during the early 1900s. The problems of the morally bankrupt Wilcox family, the honorable Schlegel family, and the victimized Bast family intertwine.

The story begins with almost no conflict or intensity (#1 through #4). The large cast of characters is introduced, and a series of coincidences bring the Schlegel, Wilcox, and Bast families together. The conflict increases when Ruth Wilcox dies, and her will is destroyed (#5). The conflict reaches an intense level when Jackie Bast reveals her past affair with Henry Wilcox (#11). The conflict reaches its greatest intensity when Charles Wilcox kills Leonard Bast (#16). In the resolution (#17), the Schlegels reside at Howards End, and the Wilcox family is shattered.

The conflict in *Howards End* is internal, not external or physical. The story is told through the emotional conflict of the characters, rather than physical events like shark attacks or car chases. The only physical conflict, motivated by an internal conflict, occurs at the story's climax when Henry Bast is killed.

Visual Structure

The terms used to describe the three basic parts of a story's structure also apply to visual structure.

Visual Exposition

Just as there's story exposition, there's also visual exposition. The story exposition defines the characters, the story situation, the location, and the time period. Story exposition sets up the basic story elements. The visual exposition defines how the basic visual components will be used to support the story.

A story begins: "Once upon a time there was a happy family." This exposition could be expanded to: "Once upon a time there was a happy family who lived in flat space with square shapes and warm colors." Now there is both story and visual exposition. Rules for photographing the family have been created.

The picture makers have used the visual exposition to provide a visual definition for the family.

The story and visual exposition should be revealed at the same time. In Steven Spielberg's *Jaws*, the musical, visual, and story exposition occur simultaneously. The audience hears ominous music (the shark's theme song), a slow moving underwater camera looks for victims (the shark's-eye view), and the shark devours an innocent swimmer (the shark is a killer). Spielberg sets up his musical, visual, and story exposition in the opening sequence of his film. The audience learns the rules for the shark's personality, music, and camera view in this exposition. The audience has received all the facts they need to begin the story.

In *Jaws*, the musical, visual, and story rules created in the exposition never change. The theme music accompanies the shark's appearance, the shark's underwater view is always photographed in the same way, and the shark continues to attack. The audience completely associates the music and camera angle with the shark so that actually showing the shark becomes unnecessary. The expositional theme music and camera angle automatically trigger fear in the audience.

The visual exposition can set up the visual structure for all the basic visual components. Any visual component can be assigned to almost any emotion, mood, situation, or character trait. Define the meaning of a visual component in the exposition in the same way that the exposition defines the personality of characters, situations, and locations in any story.

The visual rules defined in the exposition become the guidelines for everyone involved in the production. The visual component choices for space, line, shape, tone, color, movement, and rhythm will help determine the correct lenses, camera angles, locations, wardrobe, and design elements for your production. Visual rules give a production unity, style, and (through the use of contrast and affinity) visual structure.

Visual Conflict and Climax

Visual structure, like story structure, has a conflict and a climax. The basic visual components can be structured using the Principle of Contrast & Affinity to build in intensity and reach a visual climax.

The Principle of Contrast & Affinity states:

• The greater the contrast in a visual component, the more the visual intensity or dynamic increases.

• The greater the affinity in a visual component, the more the visual intensity or dynamic decreases.

More simply stated:

CONTRAST = GREATER VISUAL INTENSITY

AFFINITY = LESS VISUAL INTENSITY

Each visual component can create contrast or affinity to control visual intensity and visual structure.

A writer uses words to create story intensity. A musician uses melodies to create musical intensity, and now we have space, line, shape, tone, color, movement, and rhythm to create visual intensity.

The visual structure created by the components should parallel the intensity of the story structure. The Principle of Contrast & Affinity allows the picture maker to increase or decrease the visual intensity within a shot, from shot to shot, or from sequence to sequence.

Visual Resolution

The end of a story is called the resolution, and visual structure has a resolution, too. In a story's resolution, the conflict ends and the story's intensity decreases. The visual intensity should also decrease using the Principle of Contrast & Affinity. As affinity of the basic visual components increases, the visual intensity will decrease.

In *Jaws*, the final shot of the film is a slow-paced wide shot as the victorious survivors swim to shore. All the visual contrasts from the climax are gone, and the final shot uses only affinity.

The Visual Structure Graph

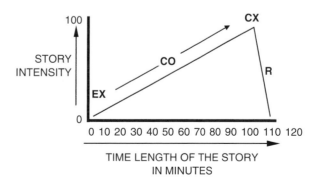

This familiar graph represents story intensity. It indicates the exposition, an intensifying conflict, a climax, and a resolution. A second graph can be added that represents the visual intensity.

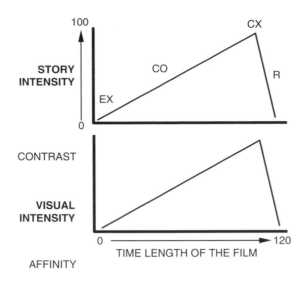

By placing a visual intensity graph directly below the story graph, the relationship between story and visuals becomes clear. The story graph indicates the story conflict intensity, and the visual intensity graph shows the amount of contrast or affinity in the visual components in direct relationship to the story. The visual intensity structure parallels the story structure. When the story structure gains intensity, the visual structure can do the same (or not, depending on your visual plan).

In this graph, the story exposition lacks intensity so the visual exposition uses affinity to keep the visual intensity low. As the story conflict begins to intensify, the visual structure does the same by increasing contrast. The story climax is most intense, so the visual climax gains the most contrast. The story intensity diminishes in the resolution and the visual structure reverts back to affinity, reducing the visual intensity. By aligning the visual graph directly under the story graph, both structures can be compared at any point along the time line of the story.

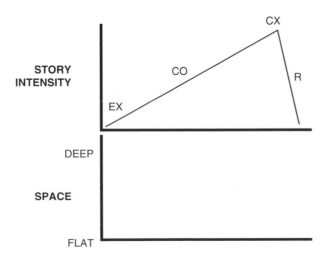

Keeping the story graph the same, the visual graph can be made more specific and useful. Instead of graphing the overall visual contrast and affinity, the second graph can be used to plan the specifics of the visual space. In this example, the visual intensity graph is labeled "flat" and "deep."

There are three variations possible for any visual component graph:

- A constant
- A progression
- Contrast or affinity

Variation #1: The Constant

As a constant, a visual component remains unchanged throughout the production.

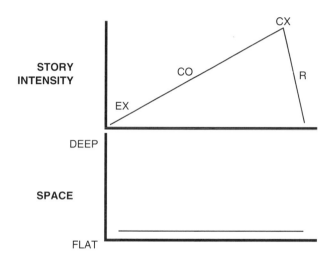

This graph indicates that the space will remain consistently flat. This production will use affinity of space. There won't be any change in the visual space of the production. Every shot will be flat.

This spatial constant is a perfect choice for certain types of stories. Perhaps this story is about a person trapped in a hopeless life with no means of escape. Keeping the space flat throughout the story helps visualize the trapped situation. This is the visual structure for Alan Pakula's film *Klute* (1972).

A story about the complicated life of a reclusive millionaire might use consistently deep space to visualize the millionaire's complex, dark inner soul. To see how that film came out, watch *Citizen Kane*.

Keeping one or more basic visual components as an unchanged constant for an entire production ensures a unity to the visual structure, because there will not be any visual component change.

Instead of keeping a visual component constant for an entire story, the component can make a gradual change or arc.

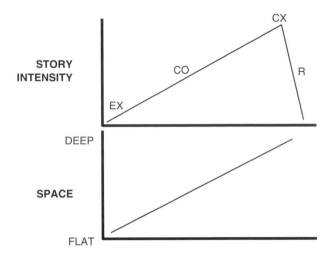

The top graph is Story and the bottom graph is Space. In this variation, the space slowly progresses, or arcs, from flat to deep. The spatial progression, or change, is motivated by the story structure.

This story is about a couple that meet, dislike each other, but end up falling in love. Flat space is assigned to dislike and deep space is assigned to love. As the story unfolds, there will be two progressions: a story progression from dislike to love, and a visual progression from flat to deep. The visual change parallels the story relationship change. The progression in the visual structure helps to tell the story and show the change in the characters' relationship.

In the story arc of *American Beauty* (1999), the family becomes increasingly dysfunctional. In *North by Northwest* (1959), the chase becomes increasingly dangerous. In *Star Wars* (1977), Luke Skywalker changes from a naive boy to a confident Jedi knight. In *The Verdict* (1982), a failed attorney regains his self-respect. In each film, the story or characters progressively change, creating an arc. A visual component change can be used to visualize this story or character change. The story and the visual progressions can be linked together.

Using the Principle of Contrast & Affinity with any visual component gives the picture maker the most specific visual control. The visuals in each sequence, scene, or shot can be structured and controlled in a precise relationship to the story structure.

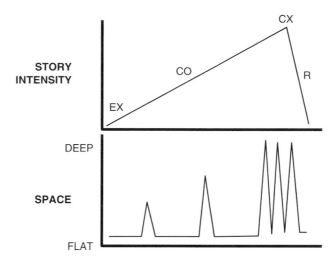

The space graph uses contrast and affinity to create a specific spatial structure that parallels the story intensity. As the story conflict increases, there are spikes of increasingly deep space. At the story's climax, there is intercutting of flat and deep space from shot to shot. The story resolution uses flat space.

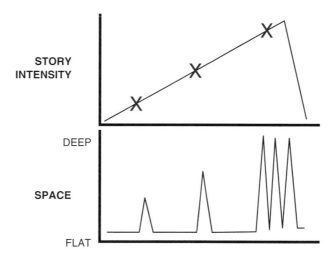

The spikes in the visual intensity graph are motivated by external conflicts found in the structure of the story intensity graph. This is a horror film about a magical hero who tracks down vampires. Vampires appear three times in the story (indicated in the story graph with an X). These appearances will be made more intense by using visual contrasts of space. The spikes in the visual structure show how the space will suddenly shift from flat to deep. The contrast between the flat and deep space adds visual intensity. The most intense part of the vampire story is a climactic fight between the hero and the vampire.

To give that sequence the greatest intensity, the space will rapidly alternate between deep and flat from shot to shot. The two graphs clearly illustrate how the story and visual intensity are linked together. The visual structure parallels the story structure.

Visual spikes are used not only for external conflicts—the spikes could heighten an internal or emotional conflict in a story. Perhaps the story is about a woman trying to remember her past. The spikes are used to create the visual intensity motivated by the woman's memories. Her thoughts can become more agitating by adding visual contrast, or more soothing by adding visual affinity. The motivation for any visual change is always found in the structure of the story.

Using the Graphs

Drawing graphs is a simple way to quickly structure the visual components. The graphs can be used to plan structures for the visual components over the course of an entire story, a sequence, one scene, or even in a single shot.

Different combinations of visual components are easy to draw and change as you find the best visual plan for your production. Try different combinations of visual components. The labels on the visual graphs can be changed, making component variations and alterations simple.

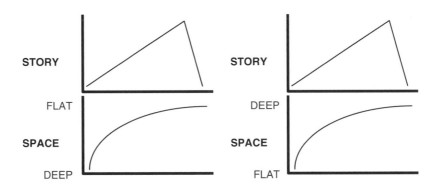

By reversing the deep and flat labels, the entire structure of space has been changed. The graphs allow quick reorganization of visual ideas. The labels placed on the graphs are arbitrary and completely flexible. They can be set up in whatever way works best for your production.

The graphs are reminders to think about each component. Creating a graph for each component reveals how the visual components will work in relation to each other and to the story structure.

It's important to remember that all visual component graphs must line up under the story graph, so the relationship between the two structures is clear.

Before the visual components can be considered, understand and graph the story structure, because the visual component's structure should support the story.

Graphs usually are produced when preparing your production. In postproduction, the graphs can be adjusted or redrawn based on an evaluation of the visual contrast and affinities in the actual footage. If you're having problems with a sequence, create graphs and analyze the edited visual structure to help find a solution to the problem.

Example #1

The graphs can diagram the structure for each visual component. Drawing a graph forces the picture maker to consider how that visual component will contribute to the visual structure and relate to the story's structure.

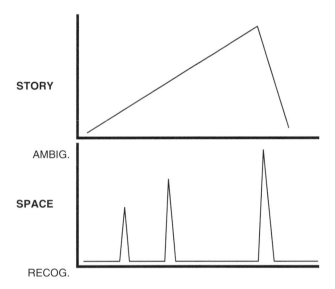

This graph indicates how ambiguous and recognizable space will be used. In this example, ambiguous space will appear three times.

This story is about a child who has frightening nightmares. Ambiguous space will be used for the dream sequences. Just as Spielberg used ominous music for the shark in Jaws, this story will use ambiguous space to indicate the child's nightmares.

The ambiguous space becomes more extreme and intense as the story progresses. The most ambiguous space will occur at the most intense part of the story's conflict, the climax. The story structure and visual structure are now linked together, so the visual intensity will grow as the story intensity increases.

Example #2

This is an action story about a detective chasing an escaped convict through a large city. The detective is passionate about justice, and the convict is a terrifying killer.

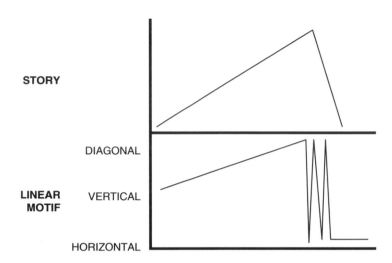

This graph, the plan for the film's linear motif, combines a progression with contrast and affinity. The linear motif begins with vertical lines and then progresses to diagonal lines. As the linear motif becomes diagonal, the story's visual sequences will gain intensity because of the viewer's emotional reaction to diagonal lines. At the climax of the story, the progression stops, and the linear motif abruptly alternates between horizontal, vertical, and diagonal lines. This visual contrast will create the greatest intensity at the story's climax. In the resolution, the convict is captured, the conflict is over, and the linear motif becomes horizontal. The structure of the linear motif has paralleled the story structure. The visuals have supported the story.

Example #3

This story is a courtroom drama. A lawyer must defend a client who is undoubtedly guilty. The lawyer struggles with the morality of the issues, and in the end justice prevails.

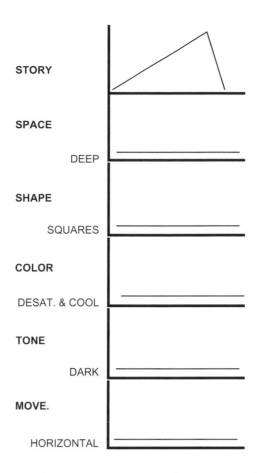

STORY

SPACE

DEEP

SHAPE

SQUARES

COLOR

DESAT. & COOL

TONE

DARK

MOVE.

HORIZONTAL

The visual rules are all constants. The visual structure will use only deep space, square shapes, cool, desaturated colors, a darker tonal range, and horizontal movement.

Keeping all, or most, of the visual components as a constant can be an excellent visual structure, if it fulfills the needs of the story. The actors will be responsible for the building conflict because the visual components will not be orchestrated to gain contrast. The affinity in the visual components will create overall visual unity, but there will not be an intensity build or climax in the visual structure.

Example #4

This is a story about farm children who run away from home, become lost in a forest, and are rescued. The idea of the story is to create a romantic portrait of rural life in the 1800s.

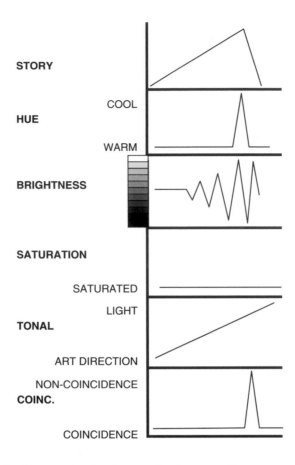

The graphing for tone and color is complex because there are many aspects to consider.

According to these graphs, the color structure is:

1. **Hue**: Warm colors with a cool spike.

2. **Tone/Brightness**: Affinity progresses to contrast.

3. **Saturation**: Remains fairly saturated.

4. **Control of Tone**: Art direction progresses to lighting.

5. **Tone**: Coincidence; noncoincidence at climax.

The terms "warm" and "cool" used in the hue graph aren't very specific. This production uses orange and yellow, which changes to yellow and cyan at the climax. Red, blue, and magenta will not be used in this production's color palette at all.

The visual components of tone and color brightness are the same, so tone is an extremely important visual component when working in color. A gray scale has been added to the brightness graph to make the tonal values more evident. Notice how the control of the tonal range shifts from reflective (art direction) to incident (lighting) control. There is also a sudden shift from coincidence to noncoincidence of tone.

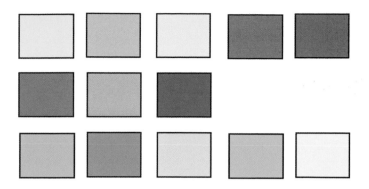

Since the graph for hue isn't specific enough, a color script has been created. The cyan and yellow colors in the bottom row are used at the cool spike indicated in the graph for hue.

Example #5

Instead of graphing an entire story, the visual component graphs can be used to plan the visual structure of a single scene. Any scene can be divided into directorial beats. A beat occurs each time there is a change in the relationship between characters or when the intention of a character changes. A beat list can substitute for a script to organize the basic visual components within a scene. A complete definition of directorial beats and the script for the following graph is included in the appendix.

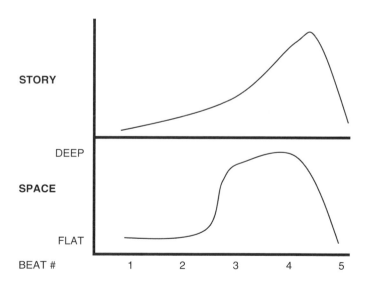

Numbers indicating the directorial beats has replaced the horizontal time line.

Detailed changes in a visual component are difficult to indicate on a graph for an entire production. This story graph is for a two-minute scene. Graphing a single scene or sequence allows the picture maker to be very specific about visual changes.

Example #6

So far, all the examples parallel the visual intensity and the story intensity. The most intense, contrasting visuals have occurred at the most intense parts of the story. But it doesn't always work that way.

Some stories have plots or character relationships where the visual components should gain affinity, not contrast. This story is about two hostile people who learn to work together in harmony.

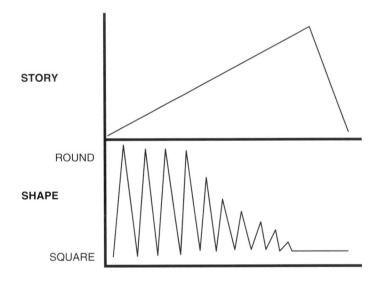

The visual component graph shows the basic shape of objects in the frame. The visual plan is to equate different shapes with the two isolated characters in the story. One character will have a square shape motif, and the other character a round motif. The contrast between square and round shapes will diminish as the story progresses. In the resolution, the characters work together, and all the shapes become square. The structure of shape is a progression that moves from contrast to affinity. The visual structure is appropriate because it visually supports the story.

Example #7

Sometimes there is no script, just a subject. The assignment is to "make something visual" and, later, music or sound effects will be added.

If there isn't any script or text, a structure is still needed as a guide for controlling the visual components.

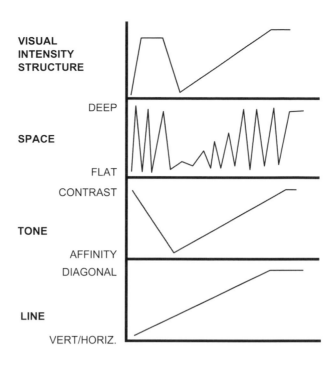

The missing story structure graph has been replaced by a graph that simply outlines the basic parts of any structure: a beginning, middle, and end. This structure graph, substituting for the story graph, becomes the guide for changes in the visual intensity. This replacement story graph might be the structure for a 10-second logo, title sequence, or television spot.

The visual component graphs of space, tone, and line gain affinity or contrast to support the structure graph. Notice how the visual components begin with intense spikes, drop in intensity, and then quickly build using contrast at the end. To make the ending have more intensity than the beginning, diagonals are introduced at the end but not used at the beginning.

Example #8

There are also situations where the visual structure must be based upon certain preexisting visual elements like stock footage, old photographs, or vintage artwork. In these cases, work backward. Instead of drawing graphs that tell you what to create, draw graphs that identify the specific visual components in the existing material. This is the only way to understand the structure you will create when the pictures are edited together. The difference between a vintage picture that you find and a new picture you take with a camera is your ability to control it. Every picture, no matter what the source, uses the same seven basic visual components in conjunction with the Principle of Contrast & Affinity.

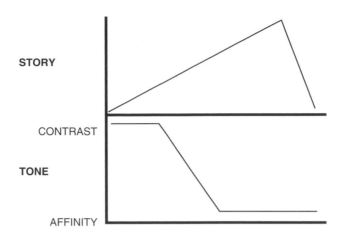

The story graph for this documentary, using vintage photographs, has a classic structure with an exposition, conflict, climax, and resolution. The tone graph is based on an analysis of the available photos that support each part of the story. The story's exposition has no intensity or conflict, but the visual exposition's photographs are extremely dynamic, full of contrast of tone. This will make the visual exposition more intense than the visual climax, which may not be the intention of the picture makers. If expositional photos with tonal affinity cannot be found, it may be possible to use other visual components to reduce the over-all intensity of the visual exposition. At the same time, other visual components can be used to add contrasts to the climax so it gains the most visual intensity.

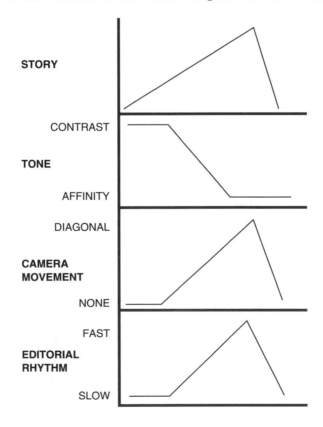

The visual components of camera movement (used to rephotograph the vintage photos) and the editorial rhythm (speed of cutting) have been structured to reduce the visual intensity of the exposition and increase the visual intensity of the climax. Remember, any visual components can become a constant, a progression, or use the Principle of Contrast & Affinity to control the visual structure.

Example #9

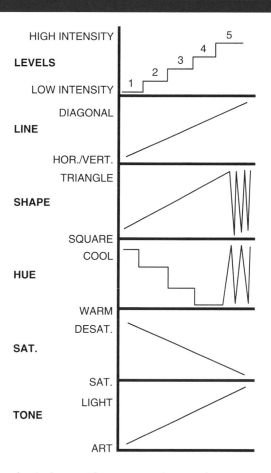

This series of graphs is for a video game. The graphs structure the five levels of the overall game. The game is structured so each new level increases the visual intensity and dynamic of the visual components. A group of more specific graphs could be created to plot the specific visual structure for each game level.

Consider each visual component when creating environments. For example, a diagonal shadow on a wall will be more intense than a horizontal shadow (or no shadow at all). If an object explodes, should the track of the flying debris move diagonally, vertically, or horizontally? Diagonal movement is most intense, but if the game is going to intensify as the player reaches new levels, the explosions might need to intensify, too. At what time of day are the events occurring and what is the weather condition? This will affect the color of light, the brightness range, and the linear motif. Controlling each visual component of the game will make its structure progress from simple to complex.

Example #10

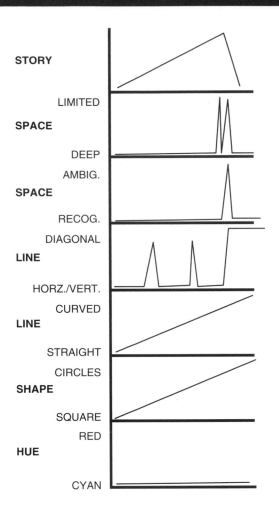

STORY

LIMITED
SPACE
DEEP

AMBIG.
SPACE
RECOG.

DIAGONAL
LINE
HORZ./VERT.

CURVED
LINE
STRAIGHT

CIRCLES
SHAPE
SQUARE

RED
HUE
CYAN

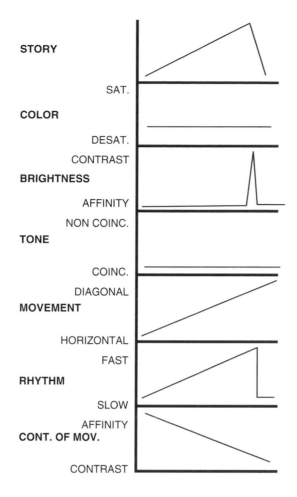

STORY

SAT.

COLOR

DESAT.

CONTRAST

BRIGHTNESS

AFFINITY

NON COINC.

TONE

COINC.

DIAGONAL

MOVEMENT

HORIZONTAL

FAST

RHYTHM

SLOW

AFFINITY

CONT. OF MOV.

CONTRAST

Here are most of the visual components graphed in relation to the story. Due to page size limitations, this series of graphs covers two pages. The story graph is repeated at the top of both pages.

Include as many graphs as your production requires. Each time a visual component is added under the story graph, it forces the picture maker to answer questions about the visual structure. The more specific the graphs become, the easier it is to stage the actors, choose locations, design sets, choose colors, place the camera, pick lenses, and decide on a lighting style.

Although this set of graphs doesn't account for all of the subcomponents, it gives a sense of the general visual controls available for any production. Here's a more comprehensive list:

1. **Story**: Intensity
2. **Space**: Flat/deep
3. **Space**: Ambiguous/recognizable
4. **Space**: Open/closed
5. **Space**: Surface divisions

6. **Line**: Quality

7. **Line**: Intensity

8. **Line**: Direction

9. **Shape**: 2D/3D

10. **Shape**: Circle, square, triangle

11. **Color**: Hue

12. **Color**: Brightness (same as Tonal Range)

13. **Color**: Saturation

14. **Color**: Warm/cool

15. **Color**: Complementary

16. **Tone**: Incident/reflectance

17. **Tone**: Coincidence/noncoincidence

18. **Movement** (object): Direction

19. **Movement** (object): Fast/slow

20. **Movement**: Continuum of movement

21. **Movement** (camera): 2D/3D

22. **Rhythm** (stationary objects): Fast/slow

23. **Rhythm** (stationary objects): Regular/irregular

24. **Rhythm** (moving objects): Fast/slow

25. **Rhythm** (moving objects): Regular/irregular

26. **Rhythm** (editorial): Fast/slow

27. **Rhythm** (editorial): Regular/irregular

28. **Rhythm**: Continuous/fragmented

The first graph is always the story structure. Since the visuals are being used to tell the story, understanding and diagramming the story intensity in detail are critical. Keep the visual structure simple. The examples in this chapter vary in complexity to demonstrate different approaches, but the best approach is often the simplest one. Although every visual component must be controlled, many can remain constant without making a change. Visual progressions and changes are important tools that should be used sparingly. An overly elaborate visual structure will be difficult to control and possibly too complex for an audience to absorb or understand.

10

Practice, Not Theory

Think about visual structure, but more importantly, use it. The graphs link story structure and visual structure together. Now, you must select the correct visual components and create the best visual structure for your production. This requires a point-of-view.

Point-of-View

The term point-of-view has a variety of meanings. Often it refers to the angle of the camera, but in this book point-of-view refers to the way that the author wants the audience to feel emotionally about the subject or story.

For example, if a writer creates a detective, the story will be written with a particular point-of-view in mind. Some examples of a point-of-view are:

- Detective as an intellectual, puzzle solving genius (Sherlock Holmes)

- Detective as a cynical, jaded loner (Sam Spade)

- Detective as a witty, wealthy socialite (Nick and Nora Charles)

- Detective as a blundering incompetent (Inspector Clouseau)

- Detective as an inappropriate, infantile pest (Ace Ventura)

In every story, the subject is a detective, but the audience feels differently about each of these detectives, because the authors had different points-of-view. The point-of-view created by the writer is a critical element of the story, because it's the main clue to choosing the visual components.

Specific points-of-view can be found in any good story. Con artists are desperate lowlifes in *The Grifters* (1990) and dapper gentlemen in *The Sting* (1973). The American cowboy is a heroic icon in *Shane* (1953) and a morally ambiguous killer in *The Unforgiven* (1992). *Dr. Strangelove* (1963), a black comedy, and *Failsafe* (1964) a tragic drama, are essentially the same story of nuclear destruction with opposite points-of-view. War is a hallucinogenic nightmare in *Apocalypse Now* (1979) and a patriotic duty in *Patton* (1969).

Becoming a champion boxer can have different outcomes and different points-of-view. In *Rocky* (1976), losing the fight creates a winning hero. In *Raging Bull* (1980), winning the fight produces a self-destructive loser. In *Million Dollar Baby* (2004), trying to win creates tragic self-sacrifice.

Television commercials always have a strong point-of-view:

- A beverage tastes great.

- A beverage is fun to drink.

- A beverage makes you an athlete.

- A beverage makes you socially desirable.

Video games have points-of-view:

- Conflicts are cute.
- Conflicts are puzzles.
- Conflicts are violent.
- Conflicts are gross.

Documentaries have points-of-view:

- A person, event, or idea is good.
- A person, event, or idea is bad.
- A person, event, or idea is fascinating.

These points-of-view have been reduced to only a word or two. The actual point-of-view for any production needs more thought and detail. A very specific point-of-view is important because it is the basis for all the decisions on any production.

Finding the point-of-view imbedded in a story is the first step to creating a visual structure. Shakespeare's plays have been presented over the last few centuries with a wide range of points-of-view, all derived from different interpretations of the same text. Most stories have a more specific point of view that a good actor, director, cinematographer, or production designer will use as a basis for their visual choices. But sometimes the story's point-of-view isn't clear. In this case, the picture maker needs to define a point-of-view, because a visual structure cannot be found without one. The picture maker must decide how the audience should feel emotionally about the story and the characters.

Choosing Components

Once a point-of-view is established, the picture maker can select visual components that best communicate that point-of-view. The approach to choosing specific visual components can vary. Four methods are instinctual, arbitrary, researched, and analytic choices.

Instinctual Choice

There are many directors, designers, and photographers who control visual structure using their instincts. Instinct is an excellent way to form a point-of-view and make visual choices. Great instincts are an inexplicable, unique talent that can solve visual structure problems.

When you first read a script or prepare with a cast and crew, there are moments of inspiration based only on your instincts. You get a flash of an idea. Something new pops into your head that solves a problem. That's when instincts are great. Use them. You may never understand why your instincts were correct, but when you see the final product you know you made the right decision.

But don't let instincts fool you. Sometimes instincts are incomplete, unreliable, or wrong. Instinctual choices may be only old habits or underdeveloped ideas that sound good but are ultimately disappointing. "If you had been there, it seemed to work" is a lame explanation for a poor instinctual choice.

If instincts collapse and inspiration is gone, understanding the basic visual components and visual structure can help you elaborate on your original instincts, make decisions, and solve visual problems.

Arbitrary Choice

You may have absolutely no idea how to choose the correct visual components. Even though you understand the definition of every component, you can't decide what choice will be best. If this is the problem, toss a coin in the air, throw darts at a list, or pick components out of a hat, but choose something, and make that arbitrary choice the visual structure.

An arbitrary choice still forces you to confront each visual component. In working with arbitrarily chosen visual components, you'll usually discover alternatives that work better, and you can then adjust and refine your choices.

The worst choice you can make is no choice at all. Remember that if you choose not to control the visual components, they will structure themselves anyway, and the audience will react to that structure based on the Principle of Contrast & Affinity. The resulting uncontrolled structure will probably work against the telling of your story.

Researched Choice

Use the work of others as a guide for visual structure. Start by reading the text, story, or script, then form a point-of-view, and look for the most appropriate visual component choices in other people's pictures.

1. Find art books with drawings, paintings, and photographs that feel correct for the visuals in your production. Don't limit yourself to pictures that deal only with your subject. Explore all kinds of pictures. Visit art museums and look at the paintings in person. If the visual components in certain pictures appeal to you, ask yourself why. What is there about the space, line, shape, tone, and color in someone else's pictures that can work for your production? You can recreate or elaborate on a borrowed visual structure. Make a scrapbook of other people's pictures that inspired your visual component choices. Give a copy of that scrapbook to your key crewmembers, so they can see what you have in mind.

2. Go to a library and read everything you can find on the subject of your project. You'll discover information that will inspire new ideas for creating visual structure.

3. Watch old movies. There are thousands of movies you haven't seen. Do some exploring. Old movies have millions of great visual ideas to borrow or

enhance. The first time you watch a movie, keep the sound turned on. If the movie looks promising for research, turn off the sound and watch it again. The more times you view it, the more details you'll notice about its visual structure.

4. Hire an artist to draw concept renderings. Work with visually creative people and dream about how your production might look. Study their drawings, because it will help you discover the visual structure for your production. In animation, dozens of artists create hundreds of conceptual drawings, exploring ways to structure the visual components. Experiment. Draw something and see how it looks.

Analytic Choice

The component choices and visual structure can be found by analyzing the text and the author's point-of-view.

A good clue to discovering the author's point-of-view is your own emotional reaction. For example, does the story make you laugh, cry, or become frightened? The written descriptions, characters, and the plot situations should communicate moods and emotions that the author wanted the audience to experience. How did the text or story make you feel? Those feelings are how you, the picture maker, should make the audience feel.

Make a list of the seven basic visual components, and consider each one as a question. What type of space is suggested by the story and its point-of-view? Often there are clues in the script. The author writes about long, narrow hallways, which would indicate longitudinal surfaces and deep space. Another location might be written as a cramped, tiny room, which suggests flat space. If the story takes place at night, how dark should it appear? Does the story suggest noncoincidence of tone, so that the subject is difficult to see, or should the subject be more coincidental and easy to see? Is there a color scheme suggested by the story? Does the author mention colors of costumes or specific locations that indicate color (forests, beaches, etc.)? Discover the correct visual components by analyzing the script.

Selecting and Controlling Visual Components

The process of selecting and controlling the visual components can be daunting. Although every visual component must be controlled, the structure of each component should be kept simple. To choose visual components, begin by answering these questions:

- What is the story?
- What is the point-of-view?
- Where is the story's location?

Here are some examples that answer these questions and lead to a visual structure.

1. **Story**: An honest, impulsive newspaper reporter infiltrates a secret society of assassins. The reporter tries to expose them, but underestimates their resources and is murdered.

2. **Point-of-View**: Dramatic and bleak. The reporter is trapped and doomed. The assassins are omnipresent, overwhelming, icy, evil, and frightening.

3. **Story Location**: Present day, a big city.

Simple answers to the three questions make finding a visual structure easier. Each visual component should communicate the emotions dictated by the point-of-view.

Space: What kind of space is bleak, evil, and frightening? There are four basic choices: deep, flat, limited, and ambiguous. Ambiguous space can make an audience feel frightened due to its lack of visual information, but it will be impossible to use ambiguous space for an entire movie.

What other type of space can create a cold, evil environment that makes the viewer feel trapped by an overwhelming presence? The answer is flat, deep or limited, because any space can be defined during the exposition as "cold and evil." The story exposition sets up the facts needed to begin the story, and the visual exposition introduces the space that will support the story. The story's emotional point-of-view will be associated with whatever space is presented on screen.

The picture makers may have a more personal approach to the space of the story. They may feel that only one particular type of space communicates bleak, trapped, and evil. Based on instinct, research, or personal taste, the picture makers decide that flat space is the only possible choice. Every shot will be flat because it is the only type of space that communicates entrapment, evil, and fear.

Line and Shape: What kinds of lines and shapes seem bleak, cold, frightening? How can line and shape convey the idea of an omnipresent assassin? The story's location is a big city, which is already full of horizontal, vertical, and square shapes. A good plan might be to emphasize the square shapes as a symbol of the assassins and eliminate diagonals and triangles.

Tone: This story is a tragedy. Darker tones might convey a dramatic, evil mood. The tonal range of this production will be limited to the lower half of the gray scale.

Color: A color scheme for this story might use only blue colors to create a cold, icy environment and mood.

Movement: A lack of camera movement might make a viewer feel trapped. Since the overall space will be flat, the actors will be physically confined, never moving in depth. All objects, including actors, will move parallel to the picture plane.

Rhythm: A slow, deliberate rhythm might create anxiety in an audience. A sudden shift of rhythm in movement and editing will create contrast, and startle or shock the viewer.

Witness (1985)

Here's another example where the story's point-of-view dictates the visual component choices., from *Witness* (1985).

1. **Story**: A farm boy, visiting a big city, accidentally witnesses a murder. A police detective protects the boy and kills the murderer.

2. **Point-of-View**: Dramatic. Farmers are good, honest, and simple. The police, except for the detective, are corrupt, dishonest, and complicated.

3. **Story Location**: A farm and a big city.

The Visual Component Plan: Because the two locations represent opposite emotional qualities, assign opposite visual components to the two basic locations:

Rural Farm: Flat space; horizontal lines; simple shapes; tonal affinity; earth colors; slow or no camera movement; slow rhythms.

Urban City: Deep space; contrasting vertical, horizontal, and diagonal lines; complex, contrasting shapes; tonal contrast; no color; hand-held and erratic camera movement; contrasting fast and slow rhythms.

Touch of Evil (1958)

Here's another visual structure based on an analysis of the story.

1. **Story**: An honest cop uncovers corruption in a small town.

2. **Point-of-View**: The unlikable characters (except for the cop), the location, and the situations are sinister, grimy, corrupt, and dangerous.

3. **Location**: A seedy little border town between Mexico and the United States.

Space: The entire film will be deep space, making the visuals dramatic and imposing. Deep space stands for the town's widespread corrupt activity.

Line and Shape: A wide range of lines and shapes will be used to give the movie visual variety. Shape differences will be emphasized, such as curved arches in contrast to rectangular doors and windows.

Tone: Every shot will exploit dark, dramatic shadows and tonal contrasts.

Movement: To increase the sense of deep space, the camera will crane and dolly, and the actors will move perpendicular to the picture plane.

Rhythm: The visual rhythms of the compositions and the editing will have as much contrast from sequence to sequence as possible. Some scenes will be filmed in a single continuous take, and others will be highly fragmented. The idea is to add visual variety and strong visual intensity to each sequence.

Something's Gotta Give **(2003)**

And finally, one more story and visual component selection.

1. **Story**: Against all odds, a confirmed playboy falls in love with a divorced woman his own age.

2. **Point-of-View**: Love is elegant, funny, and romantic.

3. **Location**: An expensive East Coast beach community and a big city.

The Visual Component Plan: This witty, intimate look at romantic relationships emphasizes the interaction of the characters. The visual components will be kept simple and visually secondary so the actors can dominate the screen.

Space: The entire film will be a mild combination of flat and limited space. Occasionally, deep space will be used to emphasize brief dramatic moments.

Line and Shape: The locations and the architecture of the sets will emphasize vertical and horizontal straight lines.

Tone: Daytime scenes will be bright and emphasize affinity. Nighttime scenes will be darker with mild contrast, emphasizing coincidence of tone. Extreme contrast will be avoided because it feels too dramatic.

Color: Brighter, desaturated blues and yellows at the beach and warm colors in the city. All colors should look inviting, nothing gloomy or sad.

Movement and Rhythm: Visual affinity.

Using Visual Structure

Making decisions about the visual components is essential to controlling visual structure. Different directors, cinematographers, and production designers work in different ways to solve the problem of finding a visual structure. Here are some suggestions for finding a method that works for you.

You can avoid planning anything and find a visual structure as you shoot one day at a time. This works well if you're fast, unusually talented, and clever. There's nothing more exciting than the moment-to-moment collaboration of cast and crew, but there's nothing more potentially disastrous as well.

Spontaneity can create unique visuals, but it's hard to maintain, difficult for coworkers to prepare or follow, and potentially unreliable.

Make notes about your plan before you get to the set. Write down ideas in your script about the meaning and point-of-view of a scene.

Translate the visual component graphs into simple reminder notes. If a component is going to gain contrast or affinity, write a note to yourself about that change. Directors often keep notes in their script about an actor's emotional state or the staging of a scene. Reminders about the visual component choices and the visual structure can also be written in the script margins. Quick notes about tonal contrast, camera movement, lens choice, or fragmentation, for example, can remind the director of the visual structure.

The earlier you begin this process the better. As you prepare, collaborate with your photographer and production designer about how to choose and control the visual components. Leave time to allow your visual ideas to mature. Then review and refine your visual structure plan. On the set, your notes will remind you to implement your visual ideas and keep your thoughts on track.

Draw storyboards. The main purpose of storyboards is to visualize shots before you shoot. If storyboards are to be of any use, they can't be taken lightly. Well-conceived storyboards are as important a commitment as the script. You may need to redraw the storyboards many times just as a writer must rewrite a script. Creating storyboards is a chance to previsualize shots and improve them. Use storyboards to discover how to compose shots, stage actors, and make use of the visual components.

Use previsualization. Pre-Viz is a software program that creates virtual sets and actors in a computer. This virtual studio provides a real-time, lens-accurate storyboard with movement that can be edited together like a finished film. There are several programs available that allow you to build virtual sets or enter measurements of locations, add moving actors, and choose accurate camera positions and lenses.

Complex action sequences for special effects films usually are tested in Pre-Viz so that problems can be solved during preparation. For his film *The Panic Room* (2002), David Fincher previsualized his entire film before he began shooting with actors on the actual sets. Spielberg used an on-set real-time Pre-Viz system to combine live action with special effects for his remake of *War of the Worlds*.

Approach the preparation process like a stage play. Assemble your actors and rehearse your production as if it were a theatre play. Since you can rehearse your entire script in real time, you'll have a unique opportunity to see the story uninterrupted from beginning to end. You won't have this view of your production again until you're in the editing room.

During this rehearsal period, you'll be able to concentrate on the story and the actors without the distractions of technical equipment and schedule restrictions. You can find the best actor staging, refine the story's point-of-view, and develop ideas for structuring the visual components.

Consider how each visual component can work to help tell your story, and what aspects of the point-of-view and the actors' performances can be underscored by a visual component.

As the rehearsals mature, key crew members can be invited to watch, and a collaborative visual structure can be developed. Camera angles can be discussed or a video camera can be used to record the rehearsals and experiment with camera angles.

Bring actors to your actual locations and videotape the rehearsals. Shoot all the necessary angles, edit it, and see if you like the results. Video cameras are inexpensive and easy to use, so producing a rehearsal version of an entire production is possible. Study this version and see how the visual components are working.

If the actors are unavailable, bring friends to your locations and take reference photos that represent the shots you'll later shoot with your actors and crew. Hand-drawn storyboards can create problems, because the drawings are often impossible to recreate with an actual camera. Taking still photos with a camera in the actual location produces a set of pictures that are more accurate than hand-drawn storyboards.

Try shooting various camera angles and decide later which ones look best. The photographs can reveal problems with the camera angles, lens choice, tone, line, shape, and color. Creating these still photos allows you to test visual component choices before shooting.

The Result

The end result of any preparation process is always the same. You're looking for ways to find a visual structure that will tell your story and express your point-of-view. In this book, most of the examples deal with stories usually found in television and theatrical features. But the principles of visual structure apply to any kind of production that appears on any kind of screen. Here are specific ways to approach visual structure depending on the kind of a production you're involved in.

The Advertisement

An ad can be a commercial, a billboard, or a magazine layout. It can appear on television, pop up on your computer, or be viewed on a hand-held digital device.

An advertisement, like any production, needs structure. It can be a traditional structure with a clearly defined exposition, conflict, climax, and resolution, or less traditional, deleting or rearranging the story structure elements. No matter what story structure is used, the visual components are employed to produce it.

An advertisement must stand out from the overwhelming competition and compel a consumer to purchase a particular product or service. Visual uniqueness often is driven by technology. As soon as a new visual trick is invented, it appears in commercials trying to grab the viewer's attention. The new visual idea will often spark a visual fad. Over the years these fads have included multiple images, split screens, soft focus, selective focus, hue and saturation manipulation, false coloring, morphing, typography and font variations, distortion lenses, letterboxing, rapid editing, stroboscopic photography, array camera photography, time lapse, slow- or fast-motion, and accelerating or decelerating movement. The visual trick appears unique, until it has been overused, and then there's a shift to the next technical discovery. Visual tricks are actually new ways to control the basic visual components.

Visuals in a commercial often take precedence over the story content. In fact, it's common for the visuals to become the content. The visuals must be carefully structured because it's not the visuals supporting a story, it's just visuals for the sake of visuals. The visual component choices become even more critical, because they are the only messengers for the point-of-view.

A car commercial can make an automobile appear sleek, quiet, and elegant by emphasizing affinity of the visual components:

Space: Flat

Line: Horizontal

Shape: Circles and curves

Tone: Middle third of the gray scale

Color: Desaturated cool colors

Camera Movement: Horizontal

Object Movement: Affinity of continuum

Rhythm: Affinity of slow, regular rhythm

The same car can be made to look speedy, loud, and wild by contrasting the visual components:

Space: Deep contrasting with flat

Line: Diagonals contrasting with horizontal

Shape: Contrast of basic shape

Tone: Contrasting tones

Color: Contrast of hue, brightness, and saturation

Movement: Contrast of two- and three-dimensional moves; contrast of continuum

Rhythm: Contrasting rhythms and cutting patterns

These visual component choices could be applied to any product or service. The Principle of Contrast & Affinity will always add or reduce visual intensity. A bar of soap has no intrinsic visual dynamic but a sports car does. By using visual component contrast, the bar of soap can be made as dynamic and intense as the sports car. On the other hand, visual affinity can reduce the intensity of any product. Photographing and editing shots of a dynamic sports car using maximum affinity will reduce or remove all the car's intrinsic intensity and make it as lifeless as the bar of soap.

Commercials and their visual cousins—identification logos, visual introductions, or titles—are brief. The standard structure of exposition, conflict, climax, and resolution can be more flexible and allow for other structures. Generally, the time length is too short for the audience to miss a changing intensity in the structure. The intensity spike at the beginning of a long form structure can be used, but can remain intense for the duration of the structure. Sustaining maximum visual intensity for 5, 10, or 15 seconds is possible if the components are carefully controlled to maintain visual contrast. Visual affinity can be used for the opposite effect.

The Documentary

Documentaries often are associated with uncontrolled circumstances, but that's not an excuse to ignore controlling the visual components. Visual structure can always be controlled, even in situations where it seems impossible.

There are three basic types of documentary productions:

- Using found footage
- Shooting in a controlled situation
- Shooting in an uncontrolled situation

Found Footage

Found footage means that the production will use only existing archival photographs, film, or video that has been shot by other people.

The first steps are to write the story, find a point-of-view, and design a visual structure that supports the story. A specific point-of-view must be defined so that the best selection of visual material can be made.

Although some documentary filmmakers recreate historical events using actors, many documentaries use vintage photographs or archival film. Analyze the visual material and define the basic visual components inherent in the pictures. The contrasts or affinities created by the visual components in the archival material will affect the visual structure of the finished production.

Re-photographing still photographs provides an opportunity for camera recomposing, camera movement, and continuum of movement. Cropping and recomposing a photograph can make it more appropriate for the point-of-view and the story's visual structure. Consider the speed of the moving camera and the lines created by its horizontal, vertical, and diagonal movement. What area of a photograph is the audience watching and where will their attention go in the next photograph? Use contrast and affinity of continuum of movement to plan the position of the photos in the frame, how they will move, and how they will be edited. Give visual structure to the archival pictures that support the story.

Because the visual material must be found, not created, control over the visual components and the Principle of Contrast & Affinity is more difficult. The graphs are still useful because they will remind the picture maker to follow a visual structure that supports the story. A boring, unstructured series of photographs cannot support a well-written script.

Controlled Documentary

A controlled documentary situation allows the picture maker to manage the visual components. Even if the documentary is full of "talking heads," a lot of control is possible. What kind of space will you place behind the talking people? What colors? What kind of lighting? What kind of lines and shapes? What lens will you use? Every basic visual component will appear in every shot. How will you use them?

The answer to these questions is point-of-view. The visual components choices will always be based on how the picture maker wants the audience feel about the subject.

A documentary, like any story, is about a conflict. The story can be traditional, depicting people in conflict (for example, wartime battles, courtroom arguments, bickering domestic situations, competing athletes, etc.).

But the definition of a conflict can be broadened for documentaries. A documentary conflict can also occur between the picture maker and the audience. The conflict becomes "will the audience understand or accept the information presented by the picture maker?" If the documentary is informational, how should the audience feel emotionally about the information they're getting? Should it be positive or negative? How the audience feels is point-of-view.

Both types of documentary must have a strong point-of-view. It may not be found until shooting is completed, but a point-of-view is critical. Without a point-of-view, there is no way of knowing how to control any of the visual components, because you won't know what emotional feelings to communicate to the audience.

Uncontrolled Documentary

Shooting a documentary in an uncontrolled situation is a difficult job because it is impossible to predict what, if anything, will happen. A clear understanding of your point-of-view can help. When something happens in an uncontrolled situation, how do you want the viewer to feel emotionally about it? You may need to develop different visual plans and have the ability to change plans quickly, depending on the situation.

Examine your shooting location carefully before you begin and try to take advantage of the visuals that are already there. Can placing the camera in a more appropriate position take advantage of visual components that are already there? Will specific lenses help to include or exclude certain visual components? The more you know about your subject and point-of-view, the easier it will be to photograph the pictures that communicate your ideas.

The most control comes in the editing room. Here, the footage can be analyzed and graphed for the basic visual components. The nature of the action in your shots will govern how the images are cut together, but be aware of the contrast and affinity in the visual components, because it will affect the viewers' emotions.

The Video Game

The only difference between a traditional story and a video game story is that the viewer has some control over the plot. This, however, does not excuse the video game creator from controlling the visual components.

Part of the experience of any video game is its structure and the progression in the game's journey or goals. The Principle of Contrast & Affinity can make the structure of the game more visually dynamic as the game progresses.

As a player advances to new levels, the game's intensifying conflict should be reflected in the visual structure. As a player gets closer to the completion (or climax) of each episode or level, the visuals should intensify or gain contrast.

All the visual components are being used in any video game, and the game players will react to the visual contrasts and affinities. Planning a visual structure, creating visual rules, and using them in a video game will greatly improve the gaming experience.

The Internet

The Internet is simply another two-dimensional surface used to show pictures containing space, line, shape, tone color, movement, and rhythm. All the visual structure ideas discussed in this book apply to every picture on the Internet.

We can carry a screen with us. This small, or sometimes tiny, screen has certain visual limitations. As the screen size shrinks, deep space becomes more difficult to create.

The computer screen's ability to show size difference is inadequate, because the average screen is small. This physical dimension severely limits the size of large objects and makes small objects difficult to see. PDA screens are even smaller. The important depth cue of size change cannot be used on tiny screens.

If all objects in a picture have the same amount of textural detail, the picture appears flat. Internet video can have this problem, depending on the resolution of the downloaded image. Tiny PDA screens have such low resolution that textural detail is unreadable.

The depth cue of tonal separation is difficult to use because video has a limited tonal range. Bright whites and dark blacks can't be reproduced because the contrast range falls outside the technical capabilities or viewing conditions of tiny screens. Black is particularly difficult to create because most video screens are viewed in brightly lit environments.

Pictures on the Internet or transmitted to PDAs cannot distinguish between subtle changes of color, and tend to reproduce similar but different colors identically. This phenomenon is called color localization and occurs in any color reproductive medium. By ignoring subtle differences in color, the screens lose depth. Color localization is discussed more completely in Chapter 6, "Color."

Multiple Camera Television Programs

Multiple cameras are used in studio and location production. Each type of production is its own world. The multicamera studio shooting style used for situation comedies, daytime dramas, game shows, and talk shows was developed in the 1950s and is still in use today.

Situation comedies and daytime dramatic programs produced in a studio are staged, designed, and photographed like a stage play inside a theatrical proscenium. The emphasis is placed on the actors, which is fine, but if you turn off the sound, you realize that the dialogue is conveying all the content. Most changes in the visual structure are minimized due to production limitations. Except for minor variations in set design, lighting, and wardrobe, these programs share an identical visual style.

Quiz shows have permanent scenery that is designed to give the program a unique look. Once designed, there is no variation from episode to episode in the visual style of these programs. Although the camera styles of different programs vary (some have more visual contrast than others), once the camera style is established, it rarely changes. The only changing element is the new contestants.

Talk shows have even less variation. Talk shows are staged flat and are copies of each other's layouts. Although each program has its own style of background scenery (color, shape, line, tone), the basic visual components remain identical from show to show. The only variation is the guest.

Location-based reality programs have an entirely different look from their studio counterparts. The physical nature of many reality programs motivates more dynamic uses of the visual components. Most reality shows replace the flat space of studio production with deep space. The wide-angle lenses used in reality television include more depth cues.

Hand-held, highly mobile cameras can easily create diagonal lines, relative movement, and rhythm shifts that are unnecessary or impossible to produce in the multicamera studio situation. Careful camera placement will force object movement perpendicular to the picture plane, which is far more dynamic than the parallel movement of situation comedies and talk shows.

The locations often shift dramatically in reality programs, so there are opportunities for constant contrasts in all the visual components. Many reality programs involve physical activity without dialogue, emphasizing the visual components in the environment instead of close-ups of talking heads.

Single-Camera Television Programs

Single-camera television shows tend to find specific rules for the visual components and then exploit those rules to make their show look unique. A program's visual style is more recognizable as the component choices become more extreme. Those choices usually involve:

- Space choices:
  a. Actors can be staged in deep or flat space.
  b. Sets and locations can be longitudinal or frontal.

- Camera choices:
  a. Dolly-mounted or hand-held camera
  b. Use of zooming lens or only fixed focal length lenses
  c. Motivated or unmotivated camera movement
  d. Slow or fast camera movement
  e. Wide angle or telephoto lenses

- Color choices:
  a. Limiting the range of hue, brightness, and saturation
  b. Adding post production effects

- Lighting choices:
  a. Light can be coincidental or noncoincidental.
  b. Tonal range can be controlled by lighting or art direction.

- Rhythm choices:
  a. Continuous or fragmented coverage style
  b. Traditional editing or unmotivated jump-cutting editorial styles

Visual style is actually a carefully chosen set of basic visual components. Specific visual component rules work well for television shows that must shoot a lot of material quickly. It's easier to make decisions because the visual component choices are purposely limited to maintain the show's style. Television shows often use different directors, so defining the visual style will help to maintain a consistent look regardless of personnel changes.

The Animated Film

It doesn't matter if your animation is traditionally hand-drawn or produced with a computer. Animation offers the greatest amount of visual control, because everything must be created. The number of visual control possibilities is far more complex, because so many more choices must be made. There is no gap between the live action world and the animation world. Both share a common visual language.

Creating graphs, defining a point-of-view, and choosing visual components is critical to the production of any hand-drawn or computer-generated imagery. Every aspect of this book relates directly to the creation of animated films, and must be used with even more control than in a live action production.

Don't Go Crazy

It's easy to overthink everything and get bogged down in visual component control. Don't let that happen—keep it simple. The clearer you can be about controlling the visual components, the easier it will be for your crew to help you and for the audience to sense the structure you had planned. You need visual rules.

It is easier to make good visual choices when there are rules to follow. If there are no rules, then there's no right or wrong answer for any question.

Think about memorable or favorite pictures you've seen on a screen. Remember that a screen is a page in a book or magazine, a billboard, a canvas in a museum, a television, a computer monitor, or a movie screen. At the foundation of all those pictures, whether the creator knew it or not, are the visual components.

Some artists, writers, directors, photographers, designers, and editors cannot explain how they chose certain visual components. Others know exactly why they did it. Which method is best? Actually, it doesn't matter at all. Whether the choice was accidental, instinctual, or carefully premeditated, it made it to the screen and it had the right effect on the audience.

What about spontaneity? Use it. Visual rules are a framework. You're not going to get arrested for breaking a visual rule, but you must keep in mind how breaking a rule will affect the audience. Don't strangle yourself with rules that make production unrealistic, but understand how and why visual structure works.

We can learn from the past. Watch old films, go to museums to view great photographs and paintings, but don't examine them with a microscope. You can be so concerned with minuscule details that the picture's overall idea becomes lost. Be careful. The audience is going to see your picture once if you're lucky, and more than once if you're extremely lucky. The audience may not notice the tiny details. Should detail be ignored and only the general visual aspects be controlled? No. But there is a middle ground where we have to be able to balance practicality with reality.

We set up rules because it helps the audience in two ways. First, they will respond to the visual unity of the film, because it will become familiar to them. When you use rules, the production takes on a specific look, or visual style. Visual style is a specific arrangement of the basic visual components.

Second, using visual rules in conjunction with the Principle of Contrast & Affinity gives the audience a visual experience that parallels the story experience. An audience wants to be taken on a ride. When they watch any screen, they want to be taken into a world that has story structure and visual structure. Even if the ride lasts only 10 seconds, they want the ride, they want the structure. Not just story structure but visual structure, too.

The Bicycle Thief, *Citizen Kane*, *Psycho*, *Die Hard*, *Cries and Whispers*, *The Godfather*, *Lawrence of Arabia*, *Manhattan*, *Saving Private Ryan*, *Rules of the Game*, *The Searchers*, *Double Indemnity*, *Yojimbo*, *Raging Bull*, Disney's *Snow White*, *The Incredibles*, your favorite video game, a great television show or commercial each has a unique look because its visual rules are so strong.

The job of the visual components is to support the story. You must know your story, understand its structure, and have a point-of-view. Linking the visual structure to the story structure allows you to motivate your visual choices. Just as a writer makes choices when writing a story, an actor makes choices when performing a role, and a musician makes choices when composing a melody, the picture maker must make choices when creating visual images. The basic visual components coupled with the Principle of Contrast & Affinity will allow you to make better pictures that communicate with an audience.

Appendix

PART A
Nodal Point Photography

Nodal point panning and tilting occur when the optical center of the lens is placed directly on axis with the pan and tilt movement of the camera.

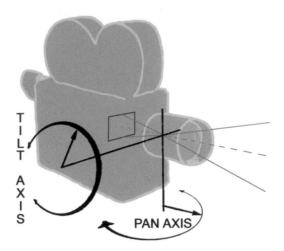

This keeps the optical center of the lens fixed as the camera is panned or tilted.

Originally developed for making camera moves in miniature and special effect photography, the nodal point tilt and pan will create absolutely no relative movement from FG to BG. Most conventional camera tripod heads are not set up for nodal point photography and will always create minor but perceptible levels of relative movement between the FG and BG.

PART B
Depth of Field: Lenses' Effects on Space

Even though wide angle lenses have a greater depth of field, all lenses have the same depth of field when the image size of the subject is kept the same.

Here's an example:

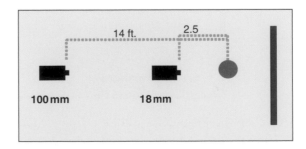

This is an overhead view or ground plan of a wall, an actor (indicated by the dot) and a camera. The camera, with a 100 mm telephoto lens, is set up 14 feet from an actor in front of a wall, but the wall is out of focus and we want both the actor and the wall to be in focus. Without moving the camera we switch to an 18 mm wide angle lens that we think "has a much greater depth of field."

Now the actor and wall are both in focus, but they're too small in the frame, so we move the camera closer to get the same image size on the actor that we had with the 100 mm telephoto lens.

When the camera is 2½ feet in front of the actor we have duplicated the image size we had with the 100 mm lens, but the wall will be out of focus again. We'll see more of the wall because the 18 mm lens's angle of view is so wide, but the wall will be as out of focus as it was with the 100 mm telephoto lens at 14 feet. All lenses have the same depth of field given the same image size.

This does not mean that wide angle lenses won't help in the creation of illusory depth. They will. But the wide angle lens will help because it forces us to place objects closer to the camera.

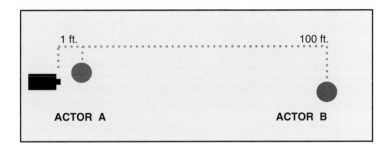

This is an overhead view or ground plan showing the camera and two actors. Note that Actor A is only 1 foot from the camera and Actor B is 100 feet from the camera.

This scene, photographed with a 15 mm wide angle lens, would look something like this:

Actor A in the foreground will be extremely large in frame and we'd see lots of detail in Actor A's face and hair. Actor B, 100 feet away in the distance, will be small in comparison and we would not see any details at all. Actor A looks biggest because Actor A is only 1 foot from the camera. Actor B is 100 feet from the camera or 10,000% further away. No wonder Actor B looks so small compared to Actor A.

Keeping the camera in the exact same place, put a 500 mm telephoto lens on the camera and look again.

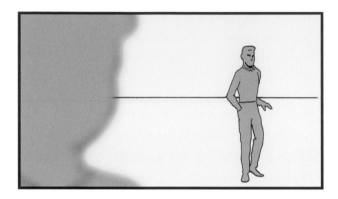

Shot #2 appears flat because there are no depth cues in the shot. Only one of the two actors will be in focus and we know that once an object is out of focus it cannot read as a depth cue. Actor A is too close to the camera and will photograph as an out-of-focus shape.

Keeping the actors in the same place, the camera with the 500 mm telephoto lens will move back 2,500 feet (roughly half a mile).

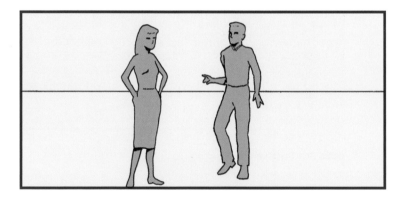

Shot #3 looks very flat. Both actors are in focus and appear almost the same size because they're both nearly the same distance from the camera. Actor A is 2,501 feet away and Actor B is 2,600 feet away. Actor B is only 4% further away than Actor A. This shot appears flat because of the distance of the objects from the camera. A telephoto lens cannot compress the image. It has no magical powers to flatten, or squash the space. The scene looks flat because all the objects in frame are relatively the same distance from the camera, which eliminates most depth cues. The telephoto lens, however, can exclude the depth cues.

Keeping the camera 2,500 feet away, a 15mm wide angle lens is put on the camera.

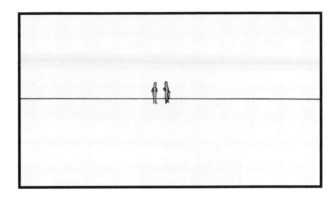

The distant actors will appear as tiny dots but if the picture is enlarged, Shot #4 will look exactly like Shot #3.

As we use longer telephoto lenses, we're forced to back the camera up in order to include and compose the objects in the frame. As we back up the camera we gain more and more distance between the camera and the objects we're photographing. This forces all in-focus objects to remain at a greater distance from the lens. When this happens, the space, due to the distance of objects from the camera, appears to flatten, but it only looks flatter because everything is equally far from the camera.

The point here is that a lens can't "compress" or "deepen" a shot. Don't depend on wide angle or telephoto lenses to create deep or flat space. The lens can help, but the creation of these two types of space will be due to the distance of objects from the camera and the lens's ability to get them into view.

Is it possible to shoot a deep space scene using a telephoto lens? Yes, although it might be easier with a wider angle lens because the wider lens can include more depth cues.

Is it possible to shoot a flat space movie with wide angle lenses? Yes, although it's sometimes easier to use a telephoto lens because it excludes the depth cues so quickly.

PART C
Anamorphic Lenses and 70mm Film

Standard lenses are called spherical or "flat" lenses. They are used to photograph the 1.33, 1.66, and 1.85 films, and all the television shows that you watch. Spherical or "flat" means that the lens's glass elements are round (not oblong or asymmetrical) and produce an image that is not distorted. (Spherical lenses are used on all still cameras.) In the early 1950s, Hollywood adopted a system that used aspherical or anamorphic lenses that purposely distorted the image. This system, first made famous by 20th Century Fox, was called Cinemascope.

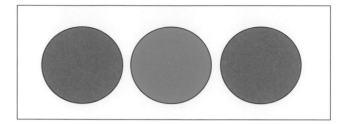

This is a 2.40:1 shot when seen through the camera's viewfinder. Using an anamorphic lens, the wide image would fit onto a standard 1.33:1 35 mm film frame.

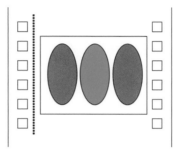

This is the same shot as it will appear on the 35 mm film. The image has been squeezed by the camera's anamorphic lens to fit onto the standard 1.33:1 35 mm film frame.

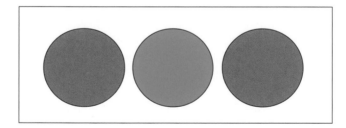

This is the same shot as it will appear on the theatre screens. The squeezed up image on the film has been unsqueezed by another anamorphic lens on the projector.

70 mm can also deliver a near 2.40:1 aspect ratio but it doesn't use anamorphic lenses. Normal, spherical lenses are used with 65 mm cameras producing an aspect ratio of 2.2:1. The release prints shown in theatres are 70 mm (5 mm wider than the 65 mm camera negative allowing space on the film for the sound track).

Most current films released in 70 mm are originally shot in 35 mm anamorphic or Super 35 mm and enlarged to 70 mm for a limited release.

PART D
The Golden Section

The Golden Section is a surface division that has long been used in classical fine art. Here are instructions on constructing a golden section based on Donald Graham's book, *Composing Pictures*.

This 2:1 frame will be divided using the golden section.

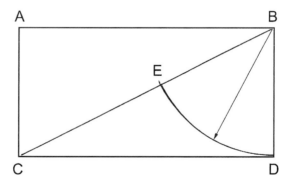

First, divide the frame in half with a diagonal line CB. Then transfer the length of the frame's side BD onto the diagonal line creating EB.

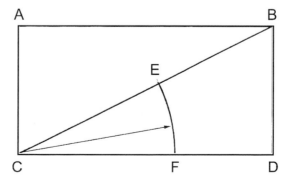

Now, transfer the length of CE down to the bottom of the frame creating point F.

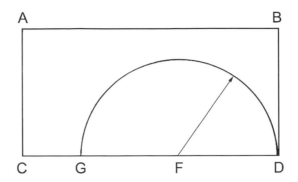

Transfer the length of FD across the bottom of the frame creating point G.

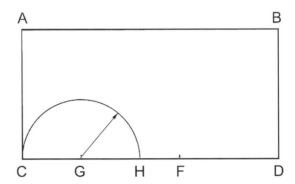

Transfer the length of CG across the bottom of the frame creating point H. Draw vertical lines from points G, H and F.

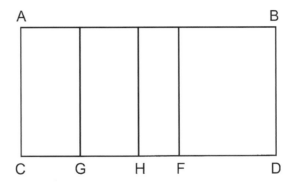

This divides the frame into four unequal parts. The proportional relation of CF to FD is called the golden section. CG is the same ratio to CF as FD is to CF. HF has the same ratio to GH as CG is to GF.

PART E

Color and Degrees Kelvin

Different light sources produce different colored light. We see most light sources as neutral white or colorless because our vision systems are able to compensate for the different colored light sources, but none of them produces white light. We can classify these various light sources with a system developed in the late 1800s by Lord William Kelvin and still in use today.

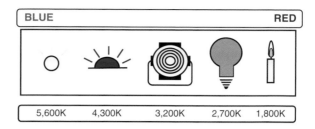

The Kelvin scale helps us describe and compare the color of light emitted from various sources. The lower the Kelvin number the redder the light, and the higher the Kelvin number the bluer the light. The scale is calibrated in degrees although these degree numbers as we use them in lighting have nothing to do with thermal heat. A 5,600 K light is not necessarily hotter than a 2,700 K light.

The Candle at 1,800 K appears fairly low on the Kelvin scale and emits a red/orange colored light. If we put candle light through a prism, it would produce a rainbow, but the rainbow would have a predominance of red/orange light.

The 60 Watt Light Bulb also produces an orange light, although not as orange as the candle. The 60 watt bulb's color temperature is approximately 2,800 K, which places it a bit closer to the blue end of the visible spectrum. A 40 watt bulb is redder (2,700 K) and a 100 watt bulb is bluer (2900 K), although any common household lightbulb gets redder with use.

The Movie Light is manufactured to emit light at 3,200 K. This is still on the redder side of the spectrum but not as red as the 60 watt bulb or the candle. The physical size or brightness of the light doesn't make any difference. If the light has been manufactured for film or video use, whether it be a 50 watt bulb or a 20,000 watt bulb, it will emit light at 3,200 K. There's one exception noted under the upcoming Daylight heading.

The Sunset in this chart has been given an arbitrary color temperature of 4,300 K. Average daylight is 5,600 K so as the sun sets, the Kelvin number continually lowers (the light gets redder) as the sun gets closer to the horizon.

Daylight on an average day at noon is approximately 5,600 K. Depending on the weather conditions, location, direction in which you are looking, and the time of year, this Kelvin reading will change. At higher altitudes where there's less atmosphere, the color temperature of skylight can get as high as 50,000 K. Daylight's color temperature has a predominance of blue and violet light although it still contains some red, yellow, and green as well. A special type of lamp was designed for film and video production to closely simulate the color of daylight. Manufactured by a variety of companies, but generically called an HMI (Hydrargyrum Medium-Arc Iodide) lamp, these lighting instruments produce a color temperature of light similar to daylight.

All the light sources mentioned so far (the sun, stage lights, household light bulbs, and candles) can be grouped together and called continuous spectrum light sources because each contains all the wavelengths of visible light in various proportions. Any continuous spectrum light source produces a visible spectrum or rainbow, although the proportions of the colors will vary depending on the light source, but all the colors will be there. Fluorescent, neon, sodium vapor, and mercury vapor lights are called discontinuous spectrum light sources because their proportion of the visible spectrum wavelengths is so irregular . For this reason, they cannot be classified on the Kelvin scale.

Light and Photography

A candle's light and daylight differ greatly in brightness and in their color. Imagine looking at a single lighted candle in a dark room and then opening a large window, allowing daylight to pour into the room. Within seconds your eyes adjust to the brightness and blue color of the daylight and everything looks "normal." Now close the window and, in the dark room, look at the candle. Its light will now appear unusually orange. Again, within seconds, your eyes will adjust and the darkness won't seem so dark and the orange candlelight will appear white.

Neither the daylight nor the candlelight is neutral white light. The daylight is too blue and the candle is too orange. They both appear neutral because our vision system has the extraordinary ability to adjust to the variations in brightness and color of most light sources. In fact, our brain constantly makes adjustments to insure we perceive what appears to be neutral, white light. These visual adjustments happen automatically just like our breathing.

Film does not have our brain's ability to adjust. Motion picture films are manufactured to be compatible (or balanced) with only two light sources. Indoor, or tungsten balanced film, is manufactured to see 3,200 K light as "normal." Outdoor, or daylight balanced film is manufactured to see 5,600 K light, as "normal." Any other combination of film and light source will change the color of the scene on film. To the human eye, both types of light look neutral because we can adjust, but film has no ability to adjust on its own.

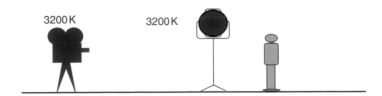

With this arrangement, the color rendition on film will be accurate. The color temperature of the film in the camera matches or balances the color temperature of the light. The color rendering on film will look normal.

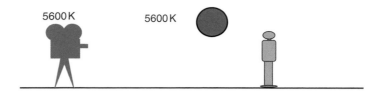

The color will remain accurate here because the film in the camera matches or balances the color temperature of the light source. The color rendering on film will be normal.

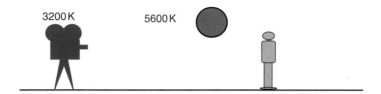

Here, the scene is outdoors in 5,600 K sunlight but with 3,200 K film in the camera. The picture will have a blue cast because the 5,600 K sunlight has a higher color temperature (bluer) than the 3,200 K light that the film is manufactured to see as normal.

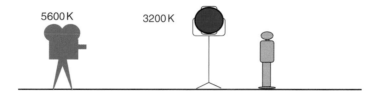

With the mismatch reversed, the 5,600 K film and a 3,200 K light source will result in an orange cast to the picture's color. The light source has a color temperature lower (redder) than the color temperature of the 5,600 K film stock.

There's a simple solution to the imbalance of lighting and film color temperatures. A filter can be added to the camera lens or the light source. The filter will change the color temperature of the light that strikes the film.

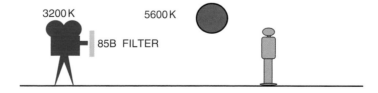

Here, an actor stands outdoors in 5,600 K sunlight. There is 3,200 K film in the camera. Shooting under these conditions will make the color on film too blue. Since the sunlight is too blue, a filter can be used to remove some of that blue light. On the subtractive color wheel, yellow is opposite blue (complementary color). Placing an orange-shish–yellow filter (commonly called an 85B filter) over the camera lens will absorb a portion of its complementary color (the unwanted blue light) and effectively lower the color temperature of the sunlight to 3,200 K.

This will balance the light source and the film. A filter absorbs its complementary color. It is subtractive because it absorbs or removes wavelengths of light. To compensate for this loss of light, the lens aperture must be opened up two-thirds of a stop (with an 85B filter) for proper exposure.

Videotape or digital storage media has no color temperature rating, but a video camera's electronics do. By activating the white balance on a camera, its electronics will compensate and make the incoming light appear neutral and white. Some video cameras can automatically white balance by reading the ambient light coming into the lens and instantaneously adjusting the video system's electronics.

Matching the color temperature of the film and light source is common practice; however, there are many times when an imbalance of the two is intentional. You might want your pictures to be too blue or orange, and so a mismatch of light and film will quickly achieve your goal. Any color shift may be artistically correct even though it's a technical mismatch between the light source and the film's color temperature. The only correct color is the color you want for your final production.

Many photographers mix color temperatures to create a more natural or varied look for a scene. In the real world we mix color temperatures all the time. A room, for example, may be lit with daylight coming though a window and a 60 watt reading lamp. We may not notice the color differences as quickly as we do on a screen, but multiple color temperatures can produce a wide variety of visual styles.

PART F
Mixing Color on Monitors

Television and computer screens do not use the additive system. The color on television and computer screens is due to a system called optical mixing, which is similar to, but different from, the additive system. Examining television and computer screens with a magnifying glass reveals that the screen is comprised of hundreds of rows of tiny red, blue, and green dots or squares. This is true for conventional tube televisions, plasma, and LCD screens. These rows look roughly like this:

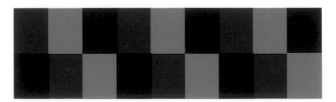

When a red color appears on screen, only the red dots light up. When a magenta color appears on the screen, both the red and blue dots brighten. When white appears on the screen, all the dots light up. The red, blue, and green dots are packed tightly together, but they do not overlap. The dots are so small that our eyes blend them together to produce color mixtures.

The additive system requires colors to overlap when mixing. Since the three colors never overlap on a television or computer screen, it can't be called additive mixing. A computer's software can be calibrated as RGB (additive) or YCM (subtractive), but the computer or television screen mixes color by optical mixing.

PART G
The Directorial Beat

The beat (a term developed in theatre) does not refer to rhythm. A directorial beat can be defined as a relationship or basic situation in a scene. A scene can be divided into many directorial beats. Each new beat signals a change in the character relationships within the scene.

This scene will illustrate directorial beats. It takes place backstage of a theatre where Jim Schreiber, a college student, looks for a rock singer named Maisy Adams.

BEAT #1:

INT. THEATRE DRESSING ROOM

Jim stands in the dressing room and looks around. Maisy enters.

MAISY   Who are you…?!
JIM   I…uh…came to see Miss Adams. Uh…the door was open.
MAISY   It still is. Close it on your way out.
JIM   Who're you?
MAISY   Her hairdresser. Now do I have to call the cops?

Jim starts to leave, stops, and closes the door.

BEAT #2:

JIM   I can't leave until she honors her commitment.
MAISY   What?
JIM   I have to tell Miss Adams: (reciting from memory). You were scheduled to do a concert at our university's Homecoming, then your manager canceled. Maybe you've received a more financially remunerative offer, but we've already advanced $7,500 for the arena and the printing of tickets. The student body and faculty are counting on me to come through. I have a responsibility to them.

MAISY   Well, you've got a real problem, kid. What makes you think I'll help you out?

BEAT #3:

Jim realizes she's Maisy Adams without her trademark green hair.

JIM   You're Maisy Adams?

MAISY   Right. Listen, I've got a show to do.

JIM   But what about the hair?

MAISY   I'm not a natural green. Look, why did you think I'd help you, anyway?

JIM   Desperation…and your lyrics. They're about treating people with love and respect and honesty. I figured you were sensitive and could understand that a decent human being could die.

MAISY   Who?

JIM   Me!

BEAT #4:

MAISY   Look, uh….

JIM   Jim. Jim Schreiber.

MAISY   You've got me feeling guilty if I sing at the other show. Then again, how do you think they'll feel if they're canceled?

JIM   I feel badly for them. But not as badly as I'd feel for myself.

MAISY   I suppose my manager could handle it. He's great in a mess; especially one he's created. You got a contract or what?

BEAT #5:

JIM   (removes contract from coat pocket) I can't tell you how happy this makes me.

MAISY   Yeah, I picked up on those vibes.

He hands her a pen.

MAISY   You know they want me to keep my real identity secret from the public.

JIM   I won't tell a soul.

She signs the contract and returns it to Jim.

JIM   Well, I'll see you next week.

MAISY   Enjoy tonight's show.

JIM   I…uh…didn't have time to purchase a ticket.

MAISY   Then watch from the wings.

Maisy takes a backstage pass off the dressing table, peels off the backing, and smoothes the sticky side onto Jim's pants leg.

Maisy smiles and Jim blushes.

END

This scene can be divided into five directorial beats. Each new beat indicates a change in the intention or relationship between Jim and Maisy.

BEAT #1: Jim is nervous and Maisy is hostile.

BEAT #2: Jim gains strength and stays.

BEAT #3: Maisy reveals her identity and Jim pleads his case.

BEAT #4: Maisy agrees; Jim is happy.

BEAT #5: Maisy flirts with Jim.

Beats are useful in a number of different ways. Writers use beats to organize a scene's plot and character relationship changes. Directors use beats to guide the actors. Beats are the key to understanding the structure of the story, the scenes, and the character relationships. There are several ways to define directorial beats.

1. **Acting**. The way the actors deliver their lines, the expressions on their faces, and their body language can delineate the beat changes. We will understand a character's change in mood, needs, and feelings if each beat is properly performed by the actor. An actor can communicate the writer's intention by understanding and using the directorial beat.

2. **Staging**. Beats can also be delineated by the staging of the actors. Each time a beat changes, the actors will rearrange themselves to show how their relationship has changed. The director will move the actors into new positions (sitting, standing, walking, etc.) in relation to each other to help communicate to the audience that the relationships or intentions have changed. Theatre relies heavily on this method of delineating beats.

3. **Camera**. The camera can be used to indicate beat changes by moving to a new position. Camera movement usually is linked to the movement of objects in the frame. As a new beat begins, the camera moves to a new position in relation to the actors. Using this method, the camera does not cut; a scene is photographed continuously.

4. **Camera/Editorial**. Assuming the scene has been fragmented, the editor is supplied with many different shots (master, two-shot, over-the-shoulder shots, close-ups, etc.) of the entire scene. This variety of shots is called "coverage." The editor examines the coverage and delineates the directorial beats by organizing the coverage.

The editor might start with a wide master for Beat #1. Beat #2 could use only the over-the-shoulder shots and Beat #3 would use only the close-ups. There are many possible variations of the scene using this approach since the scene has been photographed from so many different angles. The goal of the editor is to give the scene structure so that the beat changes are clear.

5. **Visual Component**. A beat change can be delineated by a change in a visual component. Changing the space from deep to flat for example, will help the audience sense the beat change.

In Beats #1 and #2, the dressing room might be photographed in flat space and cool colors. In Beat #3, Maisy might sit down at her dressing table and turn on the mirror lights calling attention to Jim's realization that she is the singer. At the same time the space might turn deep to help build visual conflict. Beat #5, the resolution, might have the actors move to a different area of the dressing room with a warmly colored wall in the background and a return to flat space. The more change in the visual components, the greater the intensity of the beat changes.

A director can choose one or any combination of these approaches to delineate the beat. If you delineate beats through acting and staging then you'll tend to shoot your films in a more continuous manner with fewer edits and less coverage. If you fragment your scenes and shoot coverage, you can decide in postproduction how your beat changes will be handled.

Often the method of beat delineation is determined by the schedule or limitations of the production. Television daytime dramas must shoot so much footage each day that complex staging and camera work is prohibitive. They rely on the actors for the beat delineation because it's the least time consuming.

Multicamera television sitcoms have more time to stage scenes but are limited by the live shooting style and the three-walled sets. There's more actor staging to delineate the beats but the camera angles are limited. In these situations the beats usually are delineated by the acting and the staging.

A one-camera television or theatrical film is limited only by its schedule and the talent of the production personnel in finding the best ways to control the beats.

Ignoring the beats turns a scene into long, run-on sequences that have no shape. Delineating the beats gives a scene structure, which helps the audience understand the scene.

PART H
Aspect Ratio Compatibility

When feature films are shown on television, a long-standing aspect ratio problem occurs. A 1.85 theatrical film does not fit on a conventional NTSC 1.33 television screen. There are two ways to solve the problem.

1.85 IMAGE AREA

One option is called letterboxing. The top and bottom of the 1.33 television screen are not used, allowing the film's proper aspect ratio to appear in the middle of the TV screen. The narrow black bands on the top and bottom of the 1.33 television screen alter the screen's aspect ratio to 1.85:1. Many television viewers find letterboxing unacceptable because parts of the screen are blank.

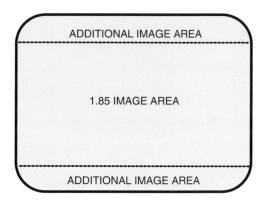

A 1.85 theatrical film can also be viewed full screen on a 1.33 television. Instead of letterboxing, the picture area above and below the 1.85 frame is revealed to accommodate the 1.33 screen. A television viewer sees the area outside the 1.85 frame, which was not projected in theatres. Although the 1.33 frame is not the proper proportion for the film's composition, the television screen is filled with a picture.

The problem becomes worse when presenting a 2.40:1 movie on a 1.33:1 television screen. There are two solutions.

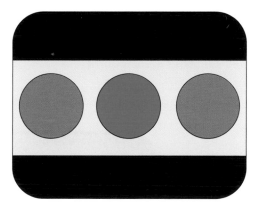

The first solution is letterboxing. A 2.40:1 aspect ratio cannot fit onto a 1.33:1 screen unless large horizontal bands at the top and bottom of the screen remain unused. General audiences won't accept letterboxing because so much of the 1.33 television screen remains blank.

The other solution is to pan and scan, which displays a portion of the 2.40:1 frame on the 1.33 television screen.

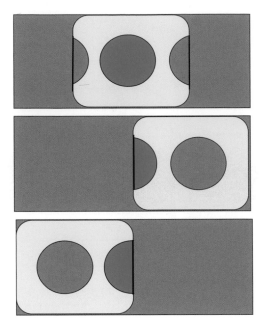

These diagrams show the three compositional choices available when a 2.40:1 film is panned and scanned for 1.33 television. The television can show only a portion of the much wider 2.40 image. In panning and scanning, the center, left, or right areas of the original 2.40 picture can be selected for 1.33 broadcast. Panning and scanning radically changes the 2.40:1 film's visual composition and may force the "pan and scan" version to appear reedited from the original film.

HDTV's aspect ratio of 16 × 9 is far more compatible with standard 1.85:1 feature films, but doesn't solve the aspect ratio problem for a 2.40:1 movie. To fit a 2:40 image on a 16 × 9 screen, the image is letterboxed, panned and scanned, or distorted to fit the screen.

The most flexible medium for aspect ratios is the Internet. Although most computer screens are 1.33:1 there are no rules or standards for the aspect ratio of original programs. Internet aspect ratios can have any shape or proportion because there are no technical limitations other than the aspect ratio and size of the computer screen.

Bibliography

Albers, Josef. *The Interaction of Color*. New Haven, CT: Yale University Press, 1963.

Alton, John. *Painting with Light*. New York: Macmillan & Co., 1949.

Arnheim, Rudolph. *Art and Visual Perception*. Berkeley, CA: University of California Press, 1954.

Arnheim, Rudolph. *Visual Thinking*. Berkeley, CA: University of California Press, 1969.

Barda, Yon. *Eisenstein: The Growth of a Cinematic Genius*. Bloomington, IN: Indiana University Press, 1973.

Bloomer, Carolyn M. *Principles of Visual Perception*. New York: Design Press, 1976.

Bouleau, Charles. *The Painter's Secret Geometry*. New York: Harcourt Brace & World, 1963.

Campbell, Joseph. *The Hero with a Thousand Faces*. New York: Pantheon Books, 1949.

Charlot, Jean. Unpublished lectures given at the Disney Studios, 1938, collection of the Disney Studio Archives.

Dean, Alexander and Carra, Lawrence. *Fundamentals of Play Directing*. New York: Holt Reinhart, Winston, 1947.

Dewey, John. *Art As Experience*. New York: Putnam, 1958.

Dewey, John. *Experience and Nature*. London: Allen & Unwin, 1929.

Dewey, John. *How We Think*. Boston: D.C. Heath, 1919.

Eisenstein, Sergei. *Film Form*. New York: Harcourt Brace & World, 1949.

Eisenstein, Sergei. *The Film Sense*. New York: Harcourt Brace & World, 1947.

Eisenstein, Sergei. *Notes of a Film Director*. London: Lawrence & Wishart, 1959.

Evans, Ralph M. *Eye, Film, and Camera in Color Photography*. London: John Wiley & Sons, 1959.

Evans, Ralph. *An Introduction to Color*. London: John Wiley & Sons, 1948.

Gibson, James J. *Perception of the Visual World*. Boston: Houghton Mifflin Co., 1950.

Gombrich, E.H. *Art and Illusion*. Princeton, NJ: Princeton University Press, 1969.

Gombrich, E.H. *The Image and the Eye*. Oxford: Phaedon Press, 1981.

Graham, Donald. *Composing Pictures*. New York: Van Reinhold Co., 1970.

Itten, Johannes. *The Art of Color*. New York: Van Nostrand Reinholt Co., 1961.

Kandinsky, Wassily. *The Art of Spiritual Harmony*. London: Constable and Co., 1914.

Katz, David. *The World of Colour*. London: Kegan Paul, Trench, Trubner & Co., 1935.

Kepes, Gyorgy, editor. *Module, Proportion, Symmetry, Rhythm*. New York: George Brazillier, 1966.

Kepes, Gyorgy, editor. *The Nature of Art and Motion*. New York: George Brazillier, 1965.

Klee, Paul. *The Thinking Eye*. New York: Wittenbourn, 1956.

Kuppers, Harald. *Color*. New York: Van Nostrand Reinhold, 1972.

Langer, Suzanne. *Problems of Art*. New York: Simon & Schuster, 1957.

Lumet, Sidney. *Making Movies*. New York: Alfred A. Knopf, 1995.

Manoogian, Haig P. *The Film-Maker's Art*. New York: Basic Books, 1966.

Merleau-Ponty, M. *Phenomenology of Perception*. London: Routledge & Kegan Paul, 1962.

Munsell, A.H. *A Color Notation*. Boston: G.H. Elis Co., 1905.

Munsell Book of Color. Glossy & Matte editions, Munsell Corporation, 1976.

Nilsen, Vladimir. *The Cinema as a Graphic Art*. London: George Newnes Ltd., 1936.

Nizhny, Vladimir. *Lessons with Eisenstein*. London: Allen & Unwin, 1962.

Ostwald, Wilhelm. *Colour Science*. London: Windsor & Newton, 1933.

Plochere, Gustov and Plochere, Gladys. *Plochere Color System*. Los Angeles, 1948.

Scharf, Aaron. *Art and Photography*. London: Jarrold & Sons Ltd., 1968.

Scientific American editors. *Communication*. San Francisco: W.H. Freeman, 1972.

Scientific American editors. *Image, Object, and Illusion*. San Francisco: W.H. Freeman and Co., 1974.

Scientific American editors. *Perception: Mechanisms and Models*.

San Francisco: W.H. Freeman and Co., 1972.

Scientific American editors. *Recent Progress in Perception*. San Francisco: W.H. Freeman and Co., 1976.

Seton, Marie. *Sergei M. Eisenstein*. New York: A.A. Wyn Inc., 1952.

Truffaut, François. *Hitchcock: A Definitive Study*. New York: Simon & Schuster, 1967.

Vernon, M.D. *A Further Study of Visual Perception*. Cambridge: Cambridge University Press, 1952.

Vorkapich, Slavko. Unpublished notes, 1950–1972, collection of University of Southern California Library.

Vorkapich, Slavko. Audio recordings of lectures, 1968–1972, collection of University of Southern California Library.

White, John. *The Birth and Rebirth of Pictorial Space*. Boston: Boston Books, 1967.

INDEX